Faith

Biblical Encounters Series

Suffering by Erhard S. Gerstenberger and Wolfgang Schrage
translated by John E. Steely
Festival and Joy by Eckhart Otto and Tim Schramm
translated by James L. Blevins
World and Environment by Odil Hannes Steck
Death and Life by Otto Kaiser and Eduard Lohse
translated by John E. Steely
Faith by Hans-Jürgen Hermisson and Eduard Lohse
translated by Douglas Stott
Achievement by Antonius H. J. Gunneweg and Walter Schmithals
translated by David Smith
Time and History by Siegfried Herrmann
translated by James L. Blevins

l

Faith

**Hans-Jürgen Hermisson
and
Eduard Lohse**

Biblical Encounters Series

Translated by Douglas W. Stott

170¹

ABINGDON

Nashville

GLAUBEN

FAITH

Library of Congress Cataloging in Publication Data
HERMISSON, HANS-JÜRGEN.
    Faith.
    (Biblical encounters series)
    Translation of Glauben.
    Includes bibliographical references.
    1. Faith—Biblical teaching—Addresses, essays,
lectures. I. Lohse, Eduard, 1924-   joint author. II.
Title. III. Series.
BS680. F27H4713   234'.2   80-22542

ISBN 0-687-12520-0

MANUFACTURED BY THE PARTHENON PRESS AT
NASHVILLE, TENNESSEE, UNITED STATES OF AMERICA

Contents

Faith

What is faith? A satisfactory answer to this question is hard to find.[1] Of course, the Christian community recites the traditional confession of faith in every worship service; but when it's time to express the content of the faith of today's Christians in one's own words, and to express it so that its present validity can be understood and accepted, words become awkward, or they fail entirely. Why is it so difficult to speak about faith so that contemporary people can understand that this question is of decisive significance for their lives? Apparently the word "faith" is one of those terms that have been so weighted down during the centuries that the original meaning now seems to be hidden. When the word "faith" is spoken, it can either precipitate critical rejection or call forth a decisive defense of traditional views, either skepticism or intolerant fanaticism. Apparently things are such—just as Paul Tillich suggested [2]—that the word faith itself must be healed before it can be used for healing people. In view of the countless misunderstandings accompanying this word, one might be inclined to avoid it entirely and attempt to describe its meaning with the help of other expressions. That, however, is virtually impossible. This word is not only protected by a powerful tradition, there is also no other term in our language capable of expressing what the word faith really means in its most fundamental sense. For this reason we must dispense with all the misinterpretations. If this task is to be completed, the question of the meaning of faith must be directed to the biblical texts in order to find out from early Christendom what it means to speak of faith. "Faith" became a central term in the theology of the early Christian communities, and particularly in Paul.

If one asks the Old Testament about the word "faith," it is initially not very talkative. The phenomenon "faith" is certainly specified, but that occurs only in rare, though significant, passages. More often, however, the Old Testament uses narrative and poetic precision instead of abstraction, and in this way it portrays the basic situations of human existence in which "faith" appears. One must then learn from the New Testament what faith "actually" means, since there one gets a conceptual orientation in spite of certain variations (or *precisely* because of such variations; since faith manifests itself from different perspectives). Such an orientation shows where one needs to look in the Old Testament if one is seeking its contribution to the understanding of faith; but one also finds much that is unique. This is presupposed in the New Testament and is simultaneously the necessary complement without which New Testament faith would be incomplete.

The contribution of the Old Testament is then above all illustrative: it shows scenes and situations in which one believes or does not believe, or in which one is called to faith, and it leads to realms of reality in which faith becomes visible. Where does faith appear, and how does it become effective? To which real experiences does faith correspond? The Old Testament answers this with stories about faith, with texts of lament and trust, and with a call to faith.

The Old Testament understanding of faith comes first in this book, not only because the Old precedes the New Testament in the Bible, but also because one can read it as a guide to the New Testament understanding of faith. The *New* Testament does not offer a different manner of faith, but faith must be articulated in a new way, and even then with the help of the Old Testament. What faith means today can still only be stated and understood with the help of the whole Bible.

A.
FAITH
IN THE
OLD TESTAMENT

I. Stories About Faith

The historical beginnings of faith lie in a past no longer accessible to us. We may suppose its roots reach back into the primal experiences of Israel's wandering ancestors; but what slowly, haltingly, is emerging here will find its articulation in the true sense only when Israel looks *back* on its past. This Israel, looking back on its past, tells us stories about its forefathers: about Abraham, Isaac, and Jacob.

These stories, however, are unique. They are not understood correctly if one considers them a more or less neutral report about things past; neither are they restricted to a particular span of time. Instead, the historical experiences of many generations are collected in such stories, which, after all, are transmitted from generation to generation and by no means remain unchanged. Each age tried to become oriented in its own world through these stories, and for that reason new experiences had to be worked into the stories about the forefathers. This was both possible and legitimate because a group's ancestor could represent the whole group, not only during his own lifetime, but for centuries thereafter. At a much later time stories could be told about Abraham which had been drawn from one's own experiences, since all later generations knew themselves to be one with Abraham. That unity of generations was realized precisely in this reverse manner by integrating one's own understanding of the world into the ancestral tradition, by articulating it within that tradition and thus really gaining it for the first time. Those stories are to be understood then as Israel's great witness to its history, encompassing large periods of time and emerging at this time, a witness through which it perpetually had to come to terms with its world and its historical experience. The richness gathered into those stories is a result of precisely this participation of numerous narrators and their respective contemporary audiences (audiences intensively participating in the creation of the stories not only as approving public, but also as the narrator's community of language and life). This is no individual, narrating here what he thought up or what he alone personally experienced and understood; this is Israel, speaking about what it encountered of its God over a period of many ages.

From the beginnings of faith Israel has spoken about its first ancestor Abraham primarily in stories, and it is characteristic for Israel's theology in general that this is *narration*, not conceptual delineation or definition. One should not view this uniqueness as the incapacity of an ancient people for conceptual distinction or as a deficiency that shows Israel to be vastly inferior, for example, to the Greek spirit. This is not at all a matter of the superiority of one ancient people or the other; and this much is certain: the peculiarity of preeminently narrative theological speech is apparently related to the uniqueness of Israel's experience of God and is attempting to be commensurate with that experience. It is, however, not Israel's only possibility, and we will encounter others in what follows (a significant example would be Israel's praise, the psalms, though admittedly here, too, with thoroughly narrative characteristics); but it is a possibility with its own justification and significance.

Israel thus comes to an understanding of faith through stories about Abraham. The famous passage about the faith that was reckoned to Abraham as righteousness (Gen. 15:6), a passage which was to play such an important role for Paul and his understanding of faith (see pp 128 ff.), does not stand at the beginning, but rather draws on a summarization gained from the stories and the "condensed" reality corresponding to them. This passage admittedly is prompts us to ask about faith in this narrative context. Here—in the formulation of a summary—there also appears the Hebraic word most closely associated with the word "to believe", namely *hä'ämin*.[3] But that is not yet an actual theological concept, and it needs to be said at the beginning that the word does not appear at all as a noun (that is—within certain limitations—nowhere in the Old Testament), but rather as a verbal term, and this usage in Genesis 15:1-6 is itself inserted into a narrative sequence. "And he believed the Lord"—the narrative account must show what this means.

From this peculiar manner of speaking about faith in the Old Testament, we can already draw some conclusions. With the word "to believe" this speech does not just mean a certain movement of the spirit, a focus or posture (though that, too, is meant), but rather over and above that a manner of behavior. (This does not mean faith in the Old Testament is a "work" in the theologically qualified sense of "good works". Such a perspective is not yet relevant, but needs rather a certain constellation of factors and later insights into the nature and possibilities of man, insights gained, to be sure, also in the Old Testament.)

1. The Promise

The Abraham stories begin with a program word by Yahweh. First there is a command to Abraham: "Go from your country and your kindred and your father's house to the land that I will show you . . . ", and to this belongs the promise: "And I will make of you a great nation, and I will bless you, and make your name great, so that you will be a blessing. I will bless those who bless you, and him who curses you I will curse; and by you all the families of the earth shall bless themselves" (Gen. 12:1-3). Within the broad context of the so-called Yahwistic layer of the Pentateuch[4] this text is the significant transition between primal history and the stories of the ancestral fathers. Whereas the narrator in that primal history (Gen. 2–11x) tells the story of man's alienation: the story of the various deficiencies in life caused by man's own willful and godless actions, and thus on the whole a story of curse *and* above and beyond that of the preservation of man in spite of it,[5] he now begins anew at just the point where the story appears to end in hopelessness. Mankind in general is no longer the theme portrayed in the acting and suffering characters, but rather a people, Israel, represented by its ancestor and patriarch Abraham. This is, of course, not just the poetic trick of a narrator whose story is threatening to run out. As a matter of fact, one should rather reverse the course of events. The point of departure is the history of his own people back to the patriarch Abraham; this people's special role, its particular relationship to its God, is the element already naturally given. But now, in the narrator's own historical situation, this is no longer enough because Israel exists in the middle of other peoples. This existence among other peoples has not only come to consciousness in the kingdom of David, it has also become that reality determining all other realms of life to an extent previously unknown. The organization of the state and its institutions, the diplomatic and cultural contacts abroad, the economy, which has been both stimulated and changed by world trade—all this may suffiice as an indication of a thoroughly changed, or at least changing, world. In this world, however, Israel had to acquire a new understanding of itself, a complicated process whose results we find in the Yahwistic work about primal history (as the history of mankind) and patriarchal history (as the beginning of Israel's history).

If one wanted to understand Israel's role among the peoples, then that primal history as a report on man's nature had to come first. It was in effect a wretched history because man is by nature wretched and wicked (cf Gen. 6:5, 8:21). However, with this new beginning in Abraham/Israel, "man" or the peoples in general are not simply overlooked or given over to the history of the curse or to an alienated existence.

Israel, granted a special role by Yahweh, was not chosen for an elite existence, but rather as a blessing for all people: the relationship to Israel will decide whether a people will win blessing or curse. That is to say: this according to the theological narrator and his matured insight is how contemporary Israel is to understand itself among the peoples: not as a nation made strong, a nation intoxicated with the power of newly acquired national greatness, and not as an old oriental people like all the others, trying intensely to imitate the customs of the great empires, but rather as the people Yahweh has taken into a particular obligation, a people that is to be *different* and is to take on a *particular* function for the peoples who experience the possibility of being drawn into Israel's salvation.

This is what the Yahwist relates in the story of Abraham, and everyone contemporary with him understood he was talking about Israel. Such understanding and agreement rests on the common conviction that the community is represented by the ancestor (as described above). Abraham is thus also thoroughly a part of the past, and is in no way only a symbol of a collective present quantity. History is peculiarly portrayed here in a way foreign to us; the present is understood as the result of a past process that begins in the past. And in this history of Abraham and his descendants, a history pointing to the present, faith is rendered *visible* as the foundation of Abrahams/Israel's existence.

A sentence about man's behavior belongs at the beginning of the story of Abraham as an imperative and promise: "So Abram went, as the Lord had told him." This sentence postulates unquestioning obedience to divine command, and to that extent appears to say nothing about faith; but it in fact accomplishes much more. It tells about human behavior based not only on a command, but simultaneously on a promise. Faith manifests itself in the human reaction to God's command *and* promise, entirely as obedience in the face of a future, promised salvation gift. But this only gives us the external outlines within which faith appears: the relationship between God and man, command and promise, and thus also the obedience that becomes involved (as opposed to mere physical obedience!).

One gets beyond this general framework by taking a closer look at the text. Three questions act as a springboard. What does the imperative demand? What is the meaning of the obedience in a larger context? And *why* does Abraham "believe"/obey?

What is demanded of Abraham? The seriousness of the imperative was immediately clear to the ancient Israelite listener. Not only is a journey into a foreign country demanded, but along with it a separation from kin and parental house, and that means from the societal connections in which man of antiquity—with the exception of the city-dwellers—was most deeply rooted. This is not only an emotional tie, but also one with a practical side. An individual's social and legal security is guaranteed by a group held together primarily by blood relationship (real or fictional). Anyone who leaves the group expects such legal insecurity, and as a stranger has elsewhere only inferior rights; he simultaneously loses the insurance of the group in the case of a threat to his economic existence, something that was indeed a threat to the life of a wanderer or to someone in a strange land. This demand thus requires that Abraham give up the basic natural human securities; from a human perspective the path leads into insecurity and uncertainty. But that is only one side of the coin. Although Abraham must leave his own country and kinship, he nonetheless goes toward a goal that will grant to him anew a country and kinship: Yahweh will make him into a great people and will Himself show him the country. Considered this way, Abraham is by no means going into the uncertain, but rather toward a highly certain and even joyous goal. But this is no longer the kind of certainty one finds among humans who are able to orient themselves according to what is already familiar, or at least visible and calculable, but rather the certainty of divine promise. Faith thus realizes itself in a movement away from the security of human life toward a future *guaranteed* only by *divine* pronouncement. Faith gives up the foundation of its own existence and wins it back again in a future qualified by the promise. It is in this context that Abraham goes forth.

Abraham's obedience acquires a special meaning within the context of primal and patriarchal history. Primal history was characterized by a chain of human error. According to the story of paradise and the fall, the activation of man's acquired capacity to differentiate between good and evil—and that means between what is good and what detrimental for man himself—leads man in fact to opt for his own ruin forever. Similarly, before and after the flood—and that means as a constant human characteristic—the narrator confirms that the human capacity for differentiation and decision in fact has done only evil (Gen. 6:5, 8:21): only with difficulty can this be understood without a reference to that motif from the story of paradise and the fall. The various deficiencies in human life, as they are portrayed in the stories of primal history, are all the result of autonomous human decisions carried out independently of God. Thus man loses his true essence wherever he emancipates himself from God.

This is *not* a question of the alternative immaturity-maturity of man in the way the post-Enlightenment interpreted the paradise story. Such interpretations have misunderstood the primal history by historicizing it, as if it were a matter of that particular moment in human history when man awoke to consciousness. This historicized misunderstanding was not circumvented by taking the story as a myth portraying the history of human development. One also misses the point if the story is understood as the development of the individual person from childhood to maturity instead of as the development of mankind in general.

Abraham's obedience is to be understood against the background of this human history just the way it is: as the history of the self-glorifying human being planning his own future and taking his fate into his own hands. The contrast is clear: Abraham does not control his own future, he lets it be controlled.[6] One might say that he retains the possibility of decision, but since he obeys and risks the undertaking he simultaneously does not opt for his own plans for the future, but rather for a divine plan. Thus, according to the Yahwistic narrator's overall concept, a history of blessing ending the history of the curse can commence with Abraham. But let us consider once more: these are not two epochs or ages standing over against one another here, but rather two ways of human life. "Natural" man, alienated from his own essential being, was portrayed in primal history, and that allows us to formulate theologically the opposing example, represented by Abraham, in the followng way: in "faith" man wins back his true being and essence.

The connection between our schematic text and primal history suggests yet another consideration. The Letter to the Hebrews mentions Noah before Abraham in the series of true witnesses of faith (Heb. 11:7; Abel and Enoch are first mentioned, but they do not concern us here because that is at any rate not the perspective of the old stories), and perhaps this corresponds to the original narrator's intention. In order to see this more clearly, we must first extract the younger Priestly narrative layer of the flood story, since it views Noah and these events from a completely different perspective. In the sections of interest to us both Genesis 6:5-8 and 7:1-5 (without v 3a) belong to the older narrative layer. The Yahwist reports there the divine annihilation decree promoted by that evil striving which begins already in one's youth. "But Noah found favor in the eyes of the Lord" (Gen. 6:8). The next section immediately discusses Yahweh's command to Noah to go into the ark, "for I have seen that you are righteous before me in this generation." A section of the Yahwistic narrative has obviously been deleted during the reworking of these two narrative layers. The command for building the ark and its execution is now given in the extensive Priestly version, which is amplified by all sorts of technical details. It has long been suspected that the older narrator understood the construction command as a test of obedience.[7] This is also not without significance for the unanswered question concerning whether in the deleted passage the command was already associated with the information about the coming flood (as is not the case in the text before us). In the final analysis, however, a hidden future would only increase the absurdity of such instructions and their execution; even when the flood was predicted it remained a bizarre risk that could be undertaken only with trust in that divine pronouncement—as was later the case for Abraham concerning the land and progeny. In any case, it thus appears we can identify related characteristics here—articulated perhaps in the phrase (although corresponding terms do not occur in the narrative context!) "characteristics of faith."

In addition, Noah is not to be taken only as a further illustrative example; the text makes its own contribution to the theme that it helps to delineate. It is in short the absolute priority of divine initiative within the constellation in which faith is to show and prove itself. Differently than in the Priestly account, in the Yahwistic account Noah is at first not excepted from the general judgment upon mankind. Thus neither in his personality nor in its good qualities can one find a motive for the words "Noah found favor." There has been much speculation concerning how Genesis 6:8 ("Noah found favor") and 7:1 ("for I have seen that you are righteous") are related; it appears certain to me that Noah's righteousness did not come first. One can then[8] see a future-orientation in 7:1: Yahweh "saw" (elected) Noah as a righteous person, namely for the preservation of the human world. But Yahweh's judgment comes as a result of an obedience in which a man let Yahweh decide the future and the behavior best corresponding to it. That is how Noah shows himself to be a precursor of Abraham and a contrasting example to that typical human behavior portrayed in the primal history. He was not the model of a better man in an otherwise totally degenerate human world, but rather was the one who followed God's call and was thus *able* to confirm faith *because* he had found grace.

From here a light falls on the beginning of the Abraham story. The point of departure is, to be sure, a different one there: not the decreed annihilation of an incorrigible humanity. But it was nonetheless a dead end for human history, and again one person was to be chosen from the many. Here, too, nothing is said about why a command and promise went out to the one giving him the possibility of faith. That divine call comes totally without mediation and encounters a person who was no better than the rest. One must read all this as an account of the patriarch and representative of one's own people. How easy it would have been to emphasize one's own good qualities, but how clearly the narrator draws attention, not to Abraham/Israel's human or ethnic merit, but rather to God. (This is also a commentary on the easily misunderstood "topos" of the Chosen People. Israel has itself understood this quite soberly.)

The last question we pose concerning Abraham's obedience is Why? We have seen that obedience was not merely self-evident in view of the command's content; one might consider such obedience in the face of a *divine* command to be something that goes without saying, but that is not the way it is portrayed here. Abraham obeys on the basis of a promise; he obeys through faith. The question must then be: Why does he *believe*? Neither the text nor its continuation offers an answer. Abraham's faith is not motivated; nothing is said about a previous relationship between God and Abraham, or even with his fathers, thus nothing is said that might allow such faith to appear comprehensible on the basis of past experience. Now, however, we must direct the question of the "why" of this faith not to the Abraham of the story, but rather to the narrator who considers himself represented in the figure of this ancestor. The narrator is Israel's spokesman. *He* knows about Israel's long history with its God, and thus for him faith is not at all blind, and it is not at all a game of chance with the unknown God who unexpectedly pops up as a numinous power.

Such an experience of power, an anonymous religious experience, although suggestive taken in and for itself, would still not be reason enough for faith. There must always be that horizon of past experiences and their having been coped with—the context in which God's new words to man take place. There must thus always be a knowledge about God, and it is always meaningless to inquire about the absolute historical beginnings of such knowledge, since every beginning itself points to something even further back. On the other hand, it is nonetheless clear that there are new, even decisively new, experiences of God in the course of such a history of the knowledge of God; thus there are certainly relative beginnings. It is just that they are often historically incomprehensible and cannot be assigned to a historical moment, but are rather the product of an entire epoch—then, perhaps, this product is formulated at a particular historical point in time.

Concerning the (relative) beginnings of faith, however, Israel has not just by chance told stories about Abraham as the prototype of faith. He is not *just* the ancestor, and even less an arbitrary symbolic figure of Israel, but is rather an example of the wandering shepherd with his flock—just as Israel's ancestors were for the most part such wandering herdsmen with sheep and goats, "small livestock nomads." In the final analysis it is the heritage of that nomadic existence that condenses itself into the concept—or initially into the narrative-circumscribing speech of faith, since the nomad needs protection in a particularly large measure: divine escort and guidance during one's travelings. This was already the case during the annual transition typical with such small livestock nomads, the transition between steppes (winter pastures) and cultivated land (summer pastures); one could never know, for example, what conditions one would encounter year after year in Palestine, a continually inhabited and politically unstable cultivated land. And it is totally the case concerning this particular instance: whenever the group must for some reason seek out completely new pasture land, whenever it must begin a journey in which life and death depend on finding water in time. Such a path into the uncertain and unsecured takes place with a trust in the protection and guidance of the deity who inspires the wandering group's leader and points out the way.[9]

Such considerations about the historical presuppositions of faith admittedly take us far beyond the textual level and its immediate statements. It is nonetheless necessary that we see how text and reality are connected, how such a text offers us neither some arbitrary phantasy nor the speculation of a theologian, but rather the condensation into language of a reality of multiple encounters filling up large periods of time. In our theologian's narrative summary we hear a chorus of many voices from many places and times.

2. Faith and Righteousness

This narrative image of the believing Abraham is by no means concluded with the portrayal of his preparation for a journey on the basis of trust in the divine pronouncement. It becomes palpable only in the following stories that all stand under the tension of the belated promise.

The Priestly text has its own peculiar image of Abraham which initially appears to contribute nothing to our topic. In its view of the history of God and man there is hardly any room for human faith, and the initiative is so emphatically pushed to God's side that only pure obedience remains for man. This is the case because the Priest carefully avoids establishing any expectation on human behavior instead of on divine deed, since the experiences of precisely this chosen people of Abraham had shown man to be incapable of such behavior. Since, then, the Priest no longer illustrates faith in all this, but rather understands that fundamental constellation God-man in a different way, we will limit our own study here to the older layer of stories. Basically the following belong to the Yahwistic layer (J): chapters 12–13; 16; 18–19. It is difficult to place chapters 15 and 22, which are important for our inquiry. While Genesis 22 is normally attributed to a somewhat later narrator, the so-called Elohist (E),[10] it has recently been suggested that Genesis 15 might not belong to the old sources at all, but reflects rather a much later theological perspective. We cannot deal with this here; but we do not need to. What is important here is the overall view of things, and that in Genesis 15 is totally in agreement with the old stories.

Genesis 15 now unites two extremely different texts, and the schematic passage about Abraham's faith (Gen. 15:6) concludes the first part. We have long known there is no old legend transmitted in Genesis 15:1-6;[11] neither is it really a story or narrative, but rather an account of a revelatory scene. God speaks to Abraham "in a vision," and Abraham answers. The dialogue is interrupted only at the end, by an external occurrence. God leads Abraham out under the night sky in order to illustrate the pronouncement; but that is only the narrative version of a common comparison: "countless as the stars."

The section is not quite unified internally (as Abraham's double speech in vv 2 and 3 shows), and yet it resists any satisfactory analysis and is intended to be taken just as it stands. The author begins with a popular transitional formulation: "After these things . . . " Many Old Testament stories begin in this way; and yet the introduction here is unique. Since Abraham left his Mesopotamian homeland some time has passed, some things have happened that have in fact brought him not one step closer to the promise of the great people; quite the contrary is the case. The initial story is followed immediately by a narrative about the journey to Egypt, which was caused by famine, a journey during which the matriarch disappears into the Pharaoh's harem—not without guilt on Abraham's part, so that a divine intervention is necessary to enable the receiver of the promise to extract himself from the affair and in the end even leave with wealth. Chapter 13 also speaks about Abraham's wealth and about the confirmation of the land pronouncement; but here, too, Abraham comes no closer to his goal. These kinds of "events" are presupposed (it is uncertain whether ch 14 is to be included), and the introductory passage covers a period of futile waiting and unfulfilled hope.

In this context there is thus now talk of a *renewal* of the promise.[12] But what is now said to Abraham: "Fear not, Abram, I am your shield; your reward shall be very great," refers on the one hand to the protection a nomad always needs, but also to the reward, and that's all Abraham refers to in his answer. "What wilt thou give me?" In this context it means: I have enough wealth, but—and this is the problem—you have given me no offspring, and I will die childless (vv 2 ff). The heir of the riches will be Abraham's house slave.

The problem articulated here must become a bit more clear. Childlessness is a tremendous misfortune, though not here in the way it was so often in the Ancient Orient (and in many parts of the world today) because then the care of the elderly parents was uncertain. Offspring, the heir: this is for Abraham more the old answer to the universally human question concerning permanence and continuance. Here, too, we find the motif of the unity of generations, not in retrospect now, but rather with a future orientation as the extension of one's own existence into a distant future by means of coming generations, grandchildren and great-grandchildren.

All this admittedly only outlines the horizon on which the question of faith is posed anew. One more thing belongs decisively in this illustrated constellation out of which faith becomes visible. On man's side one does not at all find comfortable expectation, but rather deep resignation. Abraham has already come to terms with the fact that he must accept the poor solution of the substitute heir, and he expects nothing from God and does not need to expect anything more—if one excludes childlessness as being hopeless. He can to that extent be satisfied with what he has; it is just that what is really important is missing.

The motif of the substitute solution—the fact that a different heir and progeny is being sought—occurs again in the following narrative on another level. The story of Hagar and Ishmael (Gen. 16) is nothing more than the human attempt to take things into one's own hands and move toward a solution. Human arbitrariness is again at work, so it will be an attempt which must fail in the end (in the sense of the Yahwist's understanding). The Priestly redaction picked that up later. In the great conversation between God and Abraham (Gen. 17), it has Abraham give the following answer to the promise of a son to the hundred- or ninety-year old pair: "O that Ishmael might live in thy sight!" That, too, is a form of resignation because it expresses premature diffidence or improper modesty. Here we see the sober eye for the facts, for what is humanly possible and can be put into practice. But the phenomenon of faith must always prove itself precisely where the pragmatism of human action and behavior is called into question, since that pragmatism leaves no room for the plan and historical activity of God. This will come clearly into view in Isaiah's message to his contemporaries, though it has already been brought into focus in these Abraham texts.

These characteristics let Abraham appear as anything but the one who has always been a believer. The continuing relationship to his God is certain, just as it is expressed in his resigned answer, but that is by no means yet faith (the simple assumption that there is a God would be even less an example of faith, it would be merely an inconsequential statement). Israel is not using its ancestor here to show what timeless religious perceptions are or what faith is as religious *habitus*. Neither is faith demanded equally during all periods: and wherever it is demanded, that patriarch's faith is also shown to be very much the overcoming of unbelief; to be Abraham's second answer, not the first and self-evident reaction. Here, however, the stories exhibit certain differences, human possibilities in which Israel's experiences with faith are reflected.

Resignation and pragmatism, that was the first reaction in the account of Genesis 15. Yahweh's contradiction, however, eliminates the surrogate solution. There will be no foreign heir, but rather your physical offspring, and thus the promised people Israel. "And he brought him outside and said, 'Look toward heaven, and number the stars, if you are able to number them.' Then he said to him, " 'So shall your descendants be.' " This is the renewal of the former promise, and yet even in its strengthening, it seems to contradict all probability. That illustrative reference to the stars is not meant as an aid to faith; it demands rather the most extreme willingness not to deprive oneself of that promised divine miracle.[13] One now actually expects a reaction, expects to hear Abraham's answer; but it is characteristic of this account of the revelatory scene for the narrator to forego this in favor of the concluding theological judgment. The story's flaw (though it is, as has been said, not a story at all) is no accident or result of incompetence; it blocks out any reflection about internal processes that Abraham's altered psychological disposition may have caused, and it totally blocks out any observations about the reverential gaze at the starry heaven (Israel reflected on this in another context). Those uncountable stars are there only as a visible comparison, and it is simply assumed Abraham believes. The situation is thus adequately presented, and the narrator now needs only to confirm all this. "And he believed (in) the Lord; and he reckoned it to him as righteousness."

The term we translate as "to believe" thus appears for the

first time in the Old Testament. If the author had *narrated* further, the word would have seemed out of place; he would probably have shown us rather Abraham's external behavior or his response—but not the sentence, "I believe." In the entire Old Testament this never occurs in this form—as an answer to a divine pronouncement or as the introduction to a confession of faith.[14] What then does it mean to believe?

Many critics—in a somewhat crude imitation of a differentiation made by Martin Buber[15]—are inclined to interpret this in their theologies so that real faith is a relationship of trust; the "mere" act of considering something to be true is then only a misunderstanding of what it means to "believe." Buber had tried—with a somewhat more subtle differentiation between two ways of believing—to portray the one as being uniquely Jewish, the other as specifically Christian. Accordingly, a "relationship of trust" would be characteristic of the Old Testament Jewish faith, based "on a status of contact . . . of my entirety with that in which I have trust." The New Testament Christian manner of faith is in contrast a "relationship of recognition," based "on an act of acceptance . . . by my entirety of that which I consider to be true."[16] Buber immediately emphasized—perhaps in anticipation of misunderstanding: They are based on it, but they are not it themselves. Contact in trust leads naturally to the acceptance of what proceeds from what I trust. The acceptance of what I consider true can lead to contact with that about which it gives information."[17] To this extent the difference appears to be reduced to the respective point of departure, although for Buber that is of fundamental and lasting signficance; in another context, this more simple differentiation between trusting and considering to be true would perhaps be more in order. In any case, Christian theologians have rejected and argued against this differentiation which says that Christian faith must (only) accept something as true. That rejection is certainly justified whenever one intends to say that trust is by no means merely a secondary element of Christian faith that can only be developed out of what one considers to be true. It is, however, very much a question of whether anything constructive occurred when the recognition of truth was allowed to degenerate into "considering something to be true." And it is equally questionable whether Buber performed a service by differentiating two types of faith in this way at all, whether he did not sell short the concept "to believe" in the Old Testament as well. (NB: In the whole discussion it was not a question of the content of faith and its variation, but rather the types of faith. In the final analysis, however, that is an artificial distinction which can be carried through in a only very limited fashion.) What was designated as "considering to be true" could only be an inferior mode of "truth": a conventional, perhaps more or less coerced, acceptance of "correct" statements that do not even concern me. That would no doubt have been a poor caricature of "to believe," and Buber certainly did not mean it in that way.

However, Abraham did have to consider that what Yahweh had told him was true, though now it was not a matter of just any truth, but rather of the problem at the middle of his life, or—looking back from Israel's perspective—a question of Israel's very existence. When Abraham accepted God's pronouncement as true, this was not a secondary act preceded naturally by trust. There had previously been a relationship with God, but instead of faith there was resignation on Abraham's side. Faith, however, as trust, *happened* when Abraham took God's pronouncement seriously, when he accepted it as true *in a way* that made it the determining center of his life.[18] That is admittedly only one side of the coin. We cannot limit the statement about faith to mean Abraham believed *something* Yahweh had said (the pronouncement). He "believed in the Lord" (which is the best rendering of the text), and that includes more than just the reference to words. These words of promise are only dependable if they are *simultaneously* there with the God who promises and are believed. So there is indeed an act of trust in Yahweh included in faith, but this is not just a vague, general trust, it is interpreted concretely by the words of promise. A person becoming involved with God in faith does not just participate in some vague pious feelings; that faith acquires a concrete content in this God's words about the future *because God defines himself for the believer by means of these words*. That content can then be believed in no other way than by trusting in the God who encounters man in these words and who thus renders faith possible. In a word, the differentiation between "to believe in" (trust) and "to believe that" only has theoretical analytical significance. Both in fact belong together; absolute trust must be articulated, since it is able to expect something of that in which it trusts (see below pp 102ff).

Yahweh reckons this kind of faith to Abraham as righteousness, according to the theologically reflective statement of Genesis 15:6. This formulation does not really add anything new to the interpretation of believing already given, but it does delineate it more precisely. The concept "righteousness" and its correct understanding is decisive. This is no absolute norm in the Old Testament that was already secured, but righteousness rather qualifies a relationship. Whoever behaves in a way expected of him in a given societal relationship, whoever adheres to the requirements of his society and contributes to its welfare, this person shows himself to be righteous. This becomes especially clear in conflict situations in the face of traditional rules of the society or group: not the person who adheres rigidly to the rules will be righteous, but rather the person who can also go against the rules in providing a service to the community. Such cases of conflict will admittedly always be the exception because a society's rules are indeed supposed to render possible their own unquestioned functioning and the welfare of everyone. This understanding of righteousness thus stands in total contrast to the view characterized by the motto *Fiat justitia, pereat mundus*. Righteousness is of no value in and of itself, it is to serve the world's stability. If Abraham's faith is now recognized as righteousness by God, then a term normally associated with human communities is taken over and used to describe a relationship to God. In *this* relationship between man and God, "believing", "faith", is the suitable behavior, the manner of existence corresponding to the requirements imposed on man in the relationship.

There is no particular action required of Abraham, and it may be that the statement about Abraham's righteousness in *faith* was formulated with a certain astonishment in the face of this *exception*. The normal situation from the perspective of the later people of Israel would be better expressed by the phrases in Deuteronomy 6:25: "And it will be righteousness for us, if we are careful to do all this commandment before the Lord our God, as he has commanded us." The difference between faith and works of the law (as basis for righteousness), which acquires such an enormous weight in the Pauline interpretation of the text, has not yet been brought into focus. It is not yet in focus for Abraham, to whom (as Paul argues) the Law had not yet been given, nor for those living at the time of the Yahwist, who shows Israel the model believer in Abraham, the patriarch, as the manner of existence suitable for Israel. If a later author is at work here, the fulfillment of Torah will likely have been the normal basis for Israel's righteousness as far as he was concerned, though naturally the problem had not yet arisen of competition between faith and works of the Law. Nonetheless Paul can refer to this text with good reason, since indeed nothing more was expected of Abraham here than that he willingly, and against all "real" appearances and probability, let himself take God's plans seriously, and also because this kind of fundamental determination of the relationship to God needed new and farther-reaching theological reflection under altered circumstances. And even if faith appears here as pure human passivity, let us not forget that in other contexts human action (and not just passiveness) is very much a part of things. This was already the case at the beginning of the Abraham narrative when the patriarch left his home country, and we will encounter it again, portrayed in an exemplary fashion, in the last great Abraham story (Gen. 22). Now, after the basic theological-schematic text concerning Abraham's faith, we will turn our attention to the following Abraham texts to the extent that they contribute to that portrayal of "believing".

3. Expectation and Confirmation

The portrayal of a totally different kind of divine epiphany (Gen. 15:7-21) immediately follows the revelatory scene just reported. This text also lacks unity and cannot have been the original continuation of Genesis 15:1-6. The first scene was probably consciously placed in front, rather than having been a subsequent interpretation of the peculiar occurrence. Now, however, both texts are to be read in the same context, and the statement about faith thus acquires an additional narrative interpretation. We had seen that Abraham's faith was a reaction to God's promising pronouncement; that faith had to make do with this divine donation, since no external sign was given, not even—or by no means—with that gaze at the starry heavens. But the *believing* Abraham now receives a sign of enormous significance.

If one merely takes this story in and for itself, things admittedly look different. Its point of departure is again God's pronouncement to Abraham, now with the reference to the promised land, and the divine speech encounters Abraham's thoroughly critical inquiry concerning how he is to know he will possess the land. People have often been bothered by the fact that Abraham, who just believed something "on good faith," now demands proof, and we can indeed evaluate this as well as other elements as arguments against the chapter's literary unity. Taken as a whole, however, it was hardly troublesome to the reader in antiquity that faith asks for certainty or confirmation. And in any case, the confirmation the patriarch gets is not some extraneous third element or proof coming from outside, and not even the beginning of the promised future. That proof looks rather like this:

Abraham must slaughter sacrificial animals and place their pieces across from each other in a way allowing spaces between them. Night comes (as already in v 5), and Abraham falls into a deep sleep, then a fire-epiphany passes between the pieces. God makes a covenant with Abraham through this nocturnal scene with the content: "To your descendants I give this land. . . . " Thus both are simultaneously confirmed, the promise of offspring as well as of land.

What has been gained by this peculiar ceremony? For the listener of antiquity this narrative is by no means merely speaking about weird dreams Abraham may have had while sleeping, but rather about an occurrence of the most unambiguous sort—in spite of the veiled speech. On the one hand, we see the contract ceremony with its analogical-symbolical meaning: Let he who breaches the covenant be like those animals—this is what the covenant partners announce with their path through the row of dismembered animals (cf Jer. 34:18). On the other hand, we see the fire phenomenon and Abraham, fast asleep: both stand for God's own presence. In that fire God proceeds through the row of animals, while man is only allowed to be present in a deep sleep and in that way be assured of God's presence (since man—as Israel believed—cannot endure being face to face with God). The sleeping Abraham need not obligate himself, though he attains certainty in that God personally vouches for himself. That is the proof a critical faith can expect. One can, however, view this story in another way. The fact that Israel dared at all to speak about its God in this way, that it saw its own existence so massively guaranteed by God—this itself is a characteristic of its faith.

We have already briefly mentioned what Genesis 16, the story of Hagar and Ishmael, means in this context (p 23). As is the case with all the Abraham narratives, so also with this one; they are not intended to be read only as exemplary theological stories, and certainly not as being concerned with faith only, since they contain a much larger variety of theological ideas, *and* of humanness, *and* of Israel's past. But one may just as naturally inquire of them concerning faith, since, at least collectively, they all participate in a certain image of Abraham, or more precisely: since the author of the Yahwistic editorial-layer, in spite of the kaleidoscopic material before him, nonetheless has a particular relationship between Yahweh and Abraham/Israel in mind. In Genesis 16, during the search for a substitute solution, which in fact is no solution at all, Abraham appears peculiarly inactive; his wives completely determine the action, and Abraham simply lets things go as they may. He by no means shows himself to be any sort of enthusiast for his God's plans, and he simply plays along when others are planning a practical solution. All this is simply narrated, and no judgment is made; the listener is to be left to his own thoughts.

In Genesis 18 the human reaction of unbelieving doubt is placed even farther away from Abraham than in the narrative, and Sarah must play this role in his stead. This splendid story about the visit of the three men with Abraham—who is thoroughly hospitable and after the test again received the promise of reward, namely of offspring—presents Abraham as having no faults. It was secretly a divine visit, and Abraham proved himself worthy. But both he and Sarah are now old; the birth of the heir, predicted for the coming year by one of the guests, is an impossibility and cannot go without comment. Our narrator presents that human commentary very vividly as laughter, since what is supposed to be believed is now a laughing matter (as long as one does not view it as insolence that the parent's feelings are teased in this way). Sarah, laughing, must thus serve to demonstrate the dimension of faith. Why did she laugh as if at a bad joke? And is Yahweh something that miraculous? This is how she—no, how man—with the smiling sense of superiority, is set aright by God. It is not that faith has to prove itself in the face of the impossible—no miracles are expected of the believer—but rather that he take God seriously as the one for whom nothing is "too miraculous," i.e. impossible, and that he depend on that.

This basic point is pushed to the limit in the final Abraham narrative to be discussed now. The story of Isaac's sacrifice (Gen. 22) belongs not only to the most difficult and important Old Testament stories, but also to those which have provoked the most resistance in the modern reader. There can be no question here of trying to give an appropriate interpretation.[19]

As a general aid to understanding the narrative, it must suffice here to try to remove some barriers to the modern reader so that the story again becomes readable. In the first place, the offensive element in this narrative is not to be found in the father-son relationship. That is an inviting, and not at all new, misunderstanding of a manner of portrayal that represents much more, a narrative style in which Abraham and Isaac are thus much *more* than a father and son. We must seek out that offensive element where it in fact lies, because *Israel* is speaking about its own past, in the questioning of Israel's very life and existence by Yahweh. Being the heir to the promise and existing further as the Chosen People and the offspring of Abraham are by no means unalterable facts. Israel's self-critical attitude here is echoed in John the Baptist's words about the God who "is able from these stones to raise up children to Abraham" (Matt. 3:9). And Israel experienced this kind of questioning of its existence and last-minute rescue often enough to be able to speak about it. On the other hand, this is not a narrative example of model behavior which is somehow to be imitated. The Abraham of this story could only be a "model" as an abstraction, an example of obedience to God even in extreme situations—but for this one hardly needs the example of such a narrative. Finally we need to point out that for the ancient narrator it is not the son who stands at the center of the occurrence, but rather the father, the one expected to make the sacrifice, and indeed it is a sacrifice of the future which after much waiting has finally been granted by God in a son. God puts his promise on the line—or rather, he expects man to give up all he has just received.

There is no talk at all of the feelings of the persons involved. This is characteristic of the ancient Hebrew narrative style and is part of the narrator's art, which gives the listener free rein here. But that also excludes a multiplicity of questions. For example, how did Abraham know it was really God who spoke to him? That question is explicitly answered right at the beginning of the story. Abraham's love for his son is formulated only as part of the divine command and sacrifice, and the narrator answers the question concerning Abraham's reaction to that command with an account of his unquestioning obedience. Abraham sets off just as he set off from Mesopotamia, but this time without any promise.

One can no doubt come up with all sorts of dramatic scenes for this narrative or equip it with all kinds of psychograms, and this is by no means "forbidden." One must only remain aware that this misses the intention of the original author, and one cannot extract from the narrator what one has oneself put in. (Whether one should tell this story to children is a religious-pedagogical question essentially asking whether one is able to interpret for them the actual meaning of the theologically demanding narrative.)

In the entire story there is neither explicit nor conceptual talk about faith, but there can be no question that it is to be read in this direction, since the same constellation of God, man, and future is at stake as already in Genesis 12 and 15. The theological terminology is here: God *tempted* Abraham (v 1), and Abraham proved to be God-fearing (v 12). The older version of the narrative did not yet in fact include the renewal of the old promise of blessing in verses 15-18, but rather was satisfied with the divine ascertainment of the fear of the Lord—namely of obedience that does not even refuse to offer up one's only son to God. On the other hand, the fact that God could test man was no problem for the listener in antiquity; the initial explanation rather gives him an immediate means of understanding this dark occurrence: it was only a divine testing.

But that is only the framework within which Abraham's faith is to be discussed. According to this chapter, faith is "the fear of the Lord" and thus obedience to God, but that does not exhaust its meaning—not even by pointing out that this obedience complies with an extreme demand. Abraham had already obediently followed the call out of Mesopotamia, but that was a call which opened up the future and was characterized by promises of the first order. Now, however, he follows a command without promise. If he had carried it out there would have been no more future—there would have been none possible, since God would thus have withdrawn the late realization of the promise. On what can something like faith then be based? And is this not in the final analysis simply physical obedience? Isn't everything already said about faith now called into question again?

The author of the Letter to the Hebrews formulated the basis of Abraham's faith in the following way in interpretating our text: "He considered that God was able to raise men even from the dead" (Heb. 11:19; see below pp 146-47). Even Paul had already described the patriarch's faith as grounded in the "God who gives life to the dead and calls into existence the things that do not exist" (Rom. 4:17). It is, of course, quite easy to counter that the Old Testament—with insignificant exceptions on the late fringes—knows of no such belief in resurrection and thus such hope could not be the basis of Abraham's faith, or of the author's. But this misunderstands the

intention of the New Testament interpretory statements. They
do not speak about some human hope of something desirable,
but rather about a particular power of God to which Abraham's
faith responds. It is, of course, correct to protest that the
"historical" Abraham, or rather his narrator, would not have
understood the relationship to God in this way; but this is only
of limited significance, since that interpretation is nothing more
than a crystalization of what was also addressed in the Abraham
stories, most clearly in that scolding question to the matriarch,
who is no longer laughing: "Is anything too hard for the Lord?"
(Gen. 18:14; see above pp 30-32). The answer contained there is
pushed to the limit in our narrative, and also in the New
Testament interpretations—and in view of the situation, it
must be. But one should not take this as Abraham's convenient
way out of the dilemma; the old narrative, as a matter of fact,
also did not say anything of this. But what it does mean when
Abraham acts with "the fear of the Lord" or "believing" in such
an extreme situation—and that means acting obediently *and*
with trust in his God—this is correctly interpreted in Paul and
in the Letter to the Hebrews.

Faith, according to this narrative, appears to be reduced to
pure trust, and is not a "belief that . . . " and thus does not
know God himself as any sort of content. This God does not
present himself to the believer in this story in such a way that
trust might be established. He is rather the hidden God.
Furthermore, one should not forget that this is not Abraham's
first encounter with God; God already has a history with him
determined by the promise and—contrary to all appearances—still determined by that promise. It is not the promise
that now appears withdrawn, but "only" its actual and only
realization. Saying "only" here is admittedly, from a human
perspective, intolerable, and for the Old Testament there can
in no way be talk of a spiritualization of the promised gift. But
faith is expected to make precisely this differentiation between
the promise, which is always valid because guaranteed by God,

and its—perhaps—premature, and apparently its only, possible realization. Faith is expected to see the guarantee of its realization in the God who—as Paul can then formulate it—"gives life to the dead" or, as the Old Testament put it, the God for whom "nothing is too hard"; faith is expected to seek this in the God who performs miracles.

4. Faith and Miracles

Since the emergence of the modern world-view, the problem of the biblical miracle narratives has stimulated the feelings of people in a world understood scientifically in a way that basically excludes miracles.[20] If things have become quieter today, it is not because all these questions have been answered. Nor have they been answered by science's having to limit significantly the older principles of the omnipotence of causality. Such gaps are of no value as escape hatches for the God of the Old and New Testaments because they attempt to provide for God's action with a law of statistical probability, which itself (partially) replaces the law of causality. Neither can they be answered by theology occasionally spiritualizing miracles so that miracles are only able further to exist in the new perspective on, and deeper understanding of, conditions which in fact remain the same. For example: suffering and death remain, but faith makes it possible to see everything in a new light. This is justified to a limited extent—as long as one does not make faith into an optimistic attitude or let it degenerate to the level of miracles that only help "if one believes in them." A more significant understanding of miracles, one which is totally in agreement with the biblical material, is admittedly that which sees men moved to unexpected behavior and action in faith, and thus understands miracles as having grown out of that love that is possible for believers. This should not, however, be permitted to suppress the biblical testimony to the *God* who performs miracles. This biblical witness, however, must testify more and more unambiguously to God's *omni*potence and *omni*causality, and must testify to no less than that. Here it becomes clear that Israel's and Christianity's God cannot be made into a stopgap in an apparently imperfect world-view.

When one looks back at past disputes concerning the biblical miracle narratives—much of which may now be antiquated because it was based on a misunderstanding of biblical statements—the dispute as such, is certainly not antiquated. It remains for theology to give an account of faith by considering what it means for God to act in the world, to perform miracles, and thus to render faith possible. It cannot strike all this from its repertoire without invalidating itself along with the biblical God. But to this account rendering there also belongs the clarification of just what miracles are in the Bible. They are by no means in conflict there with natural science, and thus cannot be understood as breaks in natural laws; that is a misunderstanding stemming from the confrontation between faith and natural science. There were conflicts in the Israel of antiquity as well, not concerning the question of unlimited validity of natural law, but rather concerning the fundamental problem of whether God *still* acted in the world and in history (just as he had already done in the distant past during creation, something one was able to admit and accept because to do so was inconsequential).

The question concerning God's miraculous action needs to be treated here because faith, according to the biblical understanding, refers to it as well. Just how it does this can now be examined in a narrative going beyond Abraham, a story of beginnings which is a classic for the Yahweh-faith: the narrative of the miracle at the Red Sea in Exodus 14. This narrative has been selected because it explicitly uses the Hebraic word "to believe" at the end, and in another way it is also a story of beginnings because it tells of those initial deeds of Yahweh that established Israel as a people.

The narrative sequence is generally well known and will

only be briefly recalled here. According to the account before us, Israel leaves Egypt as a great people, and although many miracles made this journey possible, Pharaoh now sets out with a chariot troop in order to bring Israel back. In the hour of greatest danger Yahweh makes a path for Israel through the sea; but the pursuing Egyptians sink into that sea, the enemies perish. All this is narrated with similarly broad lines, though with great variation in detail, in the three different sources combined together in Exodus 14. If one separates the various layers (Yahwist, Elohist, Priestly), then a heightening of the miraculous becomes unmistakable. What in the Yahwistic layer was a strong east wind driving back the sea, becomes in the priestly layer the towering walls of water on both sides of the fleeing people, who then pass through with dry feet. In the final analysis, however, this is no decisive variation. It was a miracle in any case—not just as a natural process followed by one going "against the laws of nature": Yahweh had also moved the east wind and confused the Egyptian army on the sea floor, and he then let the sea flow back in. One could perhaps more easily understand the older version as a rationalistic explanation, but it does not want to be taken in this way.

Faith is related to this miracle; before we ask about the relationship between the miracle account and the historical occurrence, we must discuss this relationship between faith and miracle according to the narrative. If one looks for the narrative's basic structure without the narrative-historical peculiarities, the following model emerges: We find Israel mortally threatened and afraid (v 10, the Yahwistic part; according to the Priestly version they cry out to Yahweh, and according to the Elohist they are murmuring against Moses[21]). Moses, however, says: "Fear not, stand firm, and see the salvation of the Lord, which he will work for you today. . . . The Lord will fight for you, and you have only to be still" (vv 13 ff). A portrayal of the events and the miraculous rescue now follows, and at the end we read: "Thus the Lord saved Israel that day . . . and Israel saw the great work which the Lord did . . . and the people *feared* the Lord; and they *believed* in the Lord and in his servant Moses" (vv 30 ff). Several elements attract attention here. Even the conclusion sounds peculiar: the faith in Moses right next to the faith in Yahweh. This shows how little the concept of faith had been fixed doctrinally, including in the religious realm. It is still associated with day-to-day usage (believing or trusting someone). In addition, this usage acquires a particular meaning within a larger context: Moses is commissioned by Yahweh to announce liberation to the people and to conduct the negotiations with the Pharaoh. He responds to this commissioning with doubt: Will they believe me? (Exod. 4:1). Yahweh shows his task to be legitimate by giving him miraculous signs, and when he has proven himself before the people in this way, "the people believed; and they heard that the Lord had visited the people of Israel and that he had seen their affliction" (Exod. 4:31). This kind of faith, brought also to Yahweh's mediator and representative, is now confirmed by Yahweh's saving act.

We need to point out that a faith-situation is already outlined at the beginning of the narrative. What faith means is portrayed almost in the manner of a model. There is fear which must be overcome, and believing now means "not to be afraid," to look at Yahweh's work and be still. "Human passivity: Yahweh acts, not man; that is how faith looks here (things will look quite similar in Isaiah, and we will have to examine that as well, but cf also Gen. 15, above pp 26 ff). The actual term admittedly does not occur until the end, and after what has already been said about faith, this is perhaps the most noticeable element.

The sequence is significant here: The people *see* the occurrence (the enemies dead on the shore), *see* Yahweh's mighty act, and then believe. According to the mode of understanding already familiar to us, we would have to ask: Why is there now faith? If one already sees, what good is faith afterward? (The well-known story of the proverbially "unbe-lieving Thomas" occurs to us, who could only be convinced by seeing and actually touching and must then hear Jesus say: "Blessed are those who have not seen and yet believe" [John 20:24-29]; see below pp 150). But this would be a misunder-standing, as if faith could make the improbable more probable and might thus be replaced or even surpassed by seeing. Furthermore, it is not a matter of faith in the miracle just experienced, but rather in the God who has demonstrated his power in such a miracle. This is a different situation than that of Abraham, since his faith must first await the miracle and is thus based on God's ability to perform miracles. Here, on the other hand, the miracle has already been seen and is, so to speak, the initial spark for faith. All this, however, may say something about the measure of faith, but very little about its essence. Abraham's faith, too, was no blind trust in an unknown God, but was based rather on past experience with a known God; it was, however, continually a matter of believing anew in the future proof of his saving power. And in a similar way the people's faith *after* the miracle is also directed toward something future. It trusts itself to its God who will accompany it through the desert and bring it into the promised land. Indeed, Israel nourished itself for centuries on the experience it had during this rescue at the Red Sea and which it subsequently articulated in narrative in this context, and it continued to refer back to it for centuries more—the most beautiful witnesses to this are found in the unknown prophet of the Babylonian exile of the sixth century, whom we call Deutero-Isaiah (cf Isa. 43:16 ff; 51:9 ff). The problem of believing and seeing, however, emerges only in a different context (see below pp 150). In the final analysis this is almost always the problem for those who no longer see or who have not themselves seen, or for those who do not yet see. This is the situation of the community removed from the saving divine acts once experienced.

But this does not exhaust our subject, and we must now

come back to the question of how miracle narrative and historical occurrence are related. When Israel looked back for centuries to these beginning events, was it not just looking at an illusion? For we know today that these events at the Red Sea just did not happen in this way. It wasn't all of Israel, but only a small group which was later absorbed into the emerging people of Israel; and it was not the entire Egyptian army, but rather only a border guard. Above all there were no walls of water for the people to go through, and that sort of thing. What the historian can ascertain about the events is this: A group of later Israelites who had fled forced labor in Egypt escaped from their pursuers when these perished in a "sea" which is now not quite accessible to us. The historian can also ascertain that those rescued understood this event as an act of their God.

Such historical insights are admittedly modest, but they are by no means insignificant. There is something to the view that something really did happen here and that Israel has not just clothed its convictions with fanciful stories. They were rescued, these refugees from Egypt. To be sure, there is much more here than can be assessed by the historian from his own presuppositions. For him it involves two things: the event and its religious interpretation. But for those actually concerned, the two were one. They did not *think* Yahweh had helped them, they *knew* it: they had experienced the event as an act of God.[22] A neutral observer may perhaps have been concerned only with the law of statistically comprehensible historical accidents, but those who were actually rescued experienced the event according to the analogy of previous encounters of faith. We must thus assign a higher value to the faith of the participants than merely that of a subsequent and somewhat late agreement. Rather, in faith that event becomes clear as a miracle, and that is a knowledge which only the believer can have, the believer who is directly affected by that event or the one to whom such an event is witnessed. Faith, however, does not add anything to the event; it only sees it as it is to be seen unedited, in its entire dimension. The clarity of correctly understood events appears in faith.

This also holds true for the oldest account of the Red Sea miracle, which precedes the source material enclosed in Exodus 14. Now, however, we are dealing with an extensive narrative in which the dimensions are overdrawn. Now, for example, all Israel is there, and finally even the walls of water. Don't we have to eliminate all that in order to catch a glimpse of the "real" miracle? That would be a false step; we must rather understand that growth from the perspective of the uniqueness of Israelite narrative. It remains rooted in reality even when all Israel appears in the story, since the participants had a determinative influence on the emerging people of Yahweh with this experience, and because the Israel of later generations was able to accommodate itself with its own experiences in that narrative of the beginnings. There were thus multiple and quite variable experiences of rescue narrated here, stylized as it were into that one basic narrative that could be repeated again and again. That heightening of the miraculous, however, is to be understood as an element of the manifold praise of the saving God. The walls of water, if one will, are nothing but a poetic stylistic element which precisely renders the dimensions of the many rescues (since poetry *is* a medium of precision).

The question concerning what the narrator and listeners themselves think "really happened" is then relatively secondary, since that introduces a category which has only limited significance for this narrative community. At the least, our isolation of individual events according to their respective dates is a procedure in which such narratives have no interest. On the contrary, they collect experiences and concentrate or focus them onto one significant point of time in the past. There is, of course, no doubt that in contrast to the Red Sea miracle, other miracle narratives cannot be questioned concerning some "historical core," but they can be questioned also concerning their relationship to that extensive reality Israel is seeking to articulate in narrative. We can only make reference to that here (and to a possibly negative result), since this can look quite different in each particular case. A genuine knowledge of reality could also be articulated in a fictionalized story.

The result was important. When faith relates itself to miracles, it is grounding itself in real events that are recognized in faith for what they are. Faith thus claims that God's realm of activity is *more* than the alleged or actual gaps in one's world-view. The biblical narrators can also make this claim in stories about pure show-miracles—in the way Yahweh gives such miracles to Moses as a means of showing himself to be legitimate (Exod. 4), or in the miraculous plagues Moses is to impose representatively on Egypt. This faith decisively relates itself, however, to Israel's experiences of rescue in which it sees at work the God who performs miracles. It makes this connection vis-à-vis its own experience or on the basis of the proclamation of Yahweh's deeds; but strictly speaking, this is no real alternative, since one's own experience is also included in the proclamation of divine action which is believed. To that extent faith in the Old Testament does relate itself to the word (cf Rom. 10, 14:17), and in fact does this in the two-fold manner, the word of proclamation of past acts of God and the word of future-oriented promise.

Two things still need to be discussed in this context. First, discontinuity with the laws of nature is of no significance whatever for the concept of miracle. It designates the extraordinary, unusual, astonishing activity of God, and that is where the involvement and certainty is expressed of those who have experienced the miracle. In the prophets one can see the possibility of speaking about God's activity by using certain "miraculous" turns of phrase without making the neutral observer leave the level of "natural" occurrences. Those prophets portray Israel's coming end as well as its rescue or eschatological reestablishment as Yahweh's deed, and variously as his direct activity in world and history. In Isaiah, for example,

Yahweh's appearance is referred to as a mighty thunderstorm; this is a quite familiar theophany motif and is for the prophet that poetic device with which he can say what *really* happened. But in virtually the same breath, he can speak about the Assyrian power which, as Yahweh's tool of judgment, rolls over Israel.

Another element belonging to the topic of faith and miracle in the Old Testament is that Israel knew, of course, that miracles do not automatically elicit faith. The Yahwist narrator formulates Yahweh's reprimand during the final uprising of the people in the desert in the following way: "How long will this people despise me? And how long will they not believe in me, in spite of all the signs which I have wrought among them?" (Num. 14:11). This presupposes that miracles are supposed to provoke faith, and within the context of the Pentateuch narrative it also very likely presupposes that they have indeed done so from time to time—the narrator says this explicitly at least on the occasion of the Red Sea miracle. But such faith was apparently not just considered to be a momentary impulse. Faith should support Israel in moments of future need and rescue as well. That, the narrator says, is what Israel did not learn in the desert when it wanted to return to Egypt after hearing the scouting reports of the "giants" in the promised land. The same motif is taken up again in Psalm 78, a long, self-critical reflection on Israel's history (vv 11, 22, 32). When we read in verse 32, "In spite of all this they still sinned; despite his wonders they did not believe," we really do not do justice to the poet's intentions if we interpret it as meaning, "The belief in God" (thus Num. 14:11) became "the act of considering his miracles to be true."[23] The linguistically shortened turn of phrase (one might also translate, "They did not believe during his miracles" or, "in spite of his miracles/wonders") means little more than the tradition reflected in it, namely that the God maintaining Israel in a miraculous manner could also expect faith when new situations arose. But Israel shows in an exemplary fashion that men can also withdraw from the evidence of miracles and thus deny the God who acts and rescues in the world.

II. Israel's Laments and the Keeping of Faith

We have already encountered the topic "the keeping of faith" several times in the narrative texts: with Abraham, when God tested him, and finally with Israel in the desert, whose faith had no stability. We could see in the model of Abraham (the "later" Abraham, and with variations) that faith as trust determines one's entire life, but it was also clear that certain situations rendered faith visible for the first time because it has to maintain itself in them and happen anew. In particular we encountered two opportunities for faith here. The one was the divine call to obedience in faith in the promise, against all appearances we well as against the apparently reasonable courses of action supported by day-to day behavioral norms. The other was characterized by danger, by a threat to existence or to the future, in general by apparently hopeless situations. This was faith within a context of danger, and we must now speak of this further.

The time of Israel's lament is the situation of danger, the time of mortal threat to the entire community or to the individual within the community. "Lament," in Israel of antiquity is a loud cry, and we may immediately ask what this has to do with faith. Nietzsche's oft-cited statement, "His disciples would have to appear more redeemed to me,"[24] apparently presupposes that lament and faith do not quite fit together. The topic of this section, however, is precisely how

they are nonetheless unalterably associated for the Old
Testament. In close proximity, then, is also the question of *how*
faith expresses itself in such texts. An important preliminary
note is that the most important Hebraic word for "to believe"
(*häʾ ämin*) only plays a very small role in the Old Testament
texts concerned here. There are only three passages to be
considered at all in which the worshiper actually speaks of his
own "faith" ("I believe that I shall see the goodness of the
Lord," Ps. 27:13, "I kept my faith," Ps. 116:10, "for I believe in
thy commandments," Ps. 119:66). In addition, the term is
found in two historical psalms, each time in an account of Israel
in the desert, already discussed in part in that context (Ps.
78:22, 32; 106:12, 24). Other linguistic forms in which faith
appears here are, however, more important for us. On the one
hand we find the series of related concepts such as "to trust"
(*batah*), "to hope" (*qiwwah*), "to preserve" (*hikkah*), "to be
protected" (*hasah*) and similar ones, and above all sentences,
images, verses, and whole pieces of poetry in which faith
expresses itself. As expressions of the believer himself (and no
longer just stories about him) these texts contribute something
new to the illustration of "believing".

As is well known, we find Israel's laments—the community as well as individual laments—for the most part in the psalms;
together with the psalms of praise (hymns and thanksgiving
psalms of the individual) they make up the main body of the
psalms collections. Some preliminary remarks need to be made
concerning the uniqueness of these texts. They are primarily
cultic texts composed for use in a worship service. What follows
from this in general is that one cannot as a rule read them as
expressions of individual feelings, nor as the direct expressions
of private spiritual life. Thus when we speak about expressions
of the believer himself, this is not to be taken in the
individualistic sense as if the private life of faith of this or that
ancient Israelite is being shown. What is characteristic is rather
a certain type of language and the fact that the specifiic

distressful situation of the person lamenting can hardly be recognized more closely—which made these texts usable on many different occasions. Instead of the expected spiritual effusion, one finds there rather a supra-individual and objectifying language. The "I" of the psalms of the individual is, as has been nicely formulated, not an individual-exclusive, but rather an inclusive I, although it is from time to time an individual person who is using these texts. The effect of such text formation is, however, not a cool distance, as one might expect, a kind of neutral portrayal of the situation, but rather an intensification of the language. In the final analysis we have here a phenomenon analogous to the textual formation of legends on which centuries have worked and which thus collect the experiences of many generations. In the language of the psalms we also find the collected power of the words of many sufferers and of many who were rescued.

It is this uniquely intensified language of the psalms, and particularly of the laments of the individual, which enables these texts to speak to us directly even today in a way equaled by only very few other Old Testament texts. They are a repertoire of the language of suffering and as such are timeless. At the same time, however, they are also texts in which faith comes to expression, and does so in direct proximity to unbelief; the language of belief and that of unbelief lie next to each other here, just as do belief and unbelief in life. Belief appears as the overcoming of unbelief in the hour of distress (note well: of one's own unbelief, although, as the texts show, the unbelief of others is also a temptation to the psalmist). We will now turn our attention to that "proximity," which in this context apparently belongs to the nature of faith.

1. Remoteness and Nearness of God

A few citations from the psalms can best show how the language of belief and that of unbelief can resemble one another to the point of being interchangeable. First the language of declared unbelief (in the believer's polemic):

> The fool says in his heart,
> "There is no God."
> They are corrupt, they do
> abominable deeds,
> there is none that does good. (14:1)
>
> In the pride of his countenance the
> wicked does not seek him;
> all his thoughts are, "There is no God . . . "
> He thinks in his heart, "God has forgotten,
> he has hidden his face, he will never see it."
>   (10:3 ff, 11)

And now the language of lament:

> "Why dost thou stand afar off, O Lord?" (10:1). "Why dost thou hide thy face? Why dost thou forget our affliction and oppression" (44:24). "How long, O Lord? Wilt thou forget me for ever? How long wilt thou hide thy face from me?" (13:2). "Why has thou forgotten me?" (42:9).

This is only a small selection from a long list of such cries of lament, and the similarity is obvious. "There is *no* God": the fool also believes this, and he does not at all mean "that higher being which he honors (not)," but rather the God acting and working in the present. His atheism is a *practiced* atheism, the God of Israel would have to act against his, the godless person's own actions. Thus by his godless action he defines the very God he denies.

As we have already noted in another context, the purely theoretical question concerning the existence of some god is insignificant here just as at all other times. It is not at all the advantage of antiquity that people then generally assumed that "there is a god." One usually differentiates here between a theoretical and a practical atheism, and antiquity in general—

with rare exceptions—is thought to have known only practical atheism. This differentiation, however, does not really seem adequate here; at least it does not yield very much, because every human practice implies a theory, which certainly can also be explicated in antiquity—just as the poet of Psalm 14 does. One would have to come up with an abstract conception of God; but neither does this kind of artificial construction yield very much, since according to the biblical understanding such a thing simply does not exist and because even today it would only be a phantom. Faith does not emerge because one becomes convinced of the existence of a god and then becomes more familiar with its specific characteristics, but rather because one has encountered the concrete God. Proofs of God's existence are then at best a secondary part of the language of faith; they might serve the reflection of faith, but for apologetics they are in principle useless.[25]

The person lamenting also speaks about God's absence. The various cries of "look here, look down here" might be added to the lament phrases already seen, since they presuppose that God in fact does not see. He is not there, is not active. That is the temptation of the person lamenting. In the face of such experience, how are the "pious" and "godless" different at this moment? They are certainly *not* different in that the pious person has decorated his world-view with the idea of God.

The difference lies initially in the fact that the lamenting person experiences God's absence in a suffering manner, while the godless person cited in our examples decrees by his own actions that God is not there, quite possibly by the kind of godless action that is affecting the person lamenting. But the difference between the oppresser and the oppressed is not really the decisive element here (also because such differences, as historical experience shows, can also be reversed in the course of time). What is essential is rather that in the face of such a similar initial situation—namely that God is not *there*—the godless do not expect that he will ever be there, while precisely this expectation is the foundation of existence for those who lament and praise in the psalms. One should not just say "for the poius" here, since that awakens images that are much too schematized. In the face of the same experience of God's remoteness, there is a small but important difference between them and the atheistic fools, and that step over into the position of the godless is neither large, nor is it merely a remote possibility for the "pious" person in temptation. The natural step is thus the advice Job receives in his misery, "Do you still hold fast your integrity? Curse God, and die" (Job 2:9). But this very cry characterizes the person calling out to the remote God, that search for God, the tense waiting, that hope even in a despairing situation. That differentiates him from the resigned, "foolish" atheist. (A word about foolishness: this naturally does not mean stupidity in the usual sense, since those cited by the poet as examples in Psalm 14 are without a doubt educated people. The Old Testament poets mean rather something to the effect "dumb in life." The "fools" do not see the foundation of all existence.)

Faith expresses itself in these psalms as that cry of lament, that expectation of the God who is now, in the hour of need, remote. Of course, this also comes to expression in the language. The believer, the person in need who turns to belief from the temptation of unbelief—he does not state anything, but rather asks: Why? How long? Is it to last forever? And he cries: Look! Turn your attention to me! But that's not all, it's not just an address to the remote God, not just an expectation directed into emptiness. We will say more about this in the next section. Here we only wanted to point out the compelling relationship between lament and faith. Martin Luther once formulated this in a sermon on Romans 5:1 ff in the following way:

> This text concludes straightaway against turning to such gossips who only want strong Christians and will tolerate no

weak ones. There is rather an eternal yearning in them, and in distress they can cry out: Abba, Father! Where one hears *that* cry, there one finds children of God. One doesn't have to be strong all the time.[26]

There the answer to Nietzsche's question to Christians is already given, and it can be found already in the prayers of lament in the Old Testament. The cry of lament to God in the expectation that God will *be* there, will be *near*, the cry that emerges in the turn from unbelief to belief: that is the sign of faith in the hour of need.

We will now see in a few examples just how this turn is carried through, or how belief expresses itself in the face of the continuing possibility of unbelief; this is where we can see that uniqueness again.

The lament naturally operates with the elements of the old world-view. One should not, however, immediately think of the etching of a swimming slice of earth with the notorious "cheese clock" above it, but should rather understand this view of the world for what it is: a reference system for man in the world, an attempt at orientation, but by no means just an object of research that one might objectify and neutrally observe— because man is a part of this world and is woven into it in an extremely intimate fashion. In the lament it sounds like this:

> Save me, O God!
>   For the waters have come up to my neck.
> I sink in deep mire,
>   Where there is no foothold;
> I have come into deep waters,
>   and the flood sweeps over me.
>
>   (69:1-2)

This is by no means talking about danger at sea; the person lamenting is about to fall away from the world and sink into the realm of chaotic primal floods. The "world" is understood as a realm of life extracted and held aloft over that chaos, a realm in which life is made possible by functioning processes and order

into which man himself fits; but wherever life is in great
danger—no matter what the reason—man falls into the realm of
the chaotic, outside the world, as portrayed by the flood
metaphor. That chaotic flood, in relation to the world structure
(or better, to the securely functioning world), must as a cosmic
quantity remain "outside," and thus becomes the articulation of
that lethal threat to everything that no longer exists in its own
normal world. This becomes comprehensible if one understands "world" as the referential quantity of human existence,
and no longer as merely a given space. The person lamenting
"outside the world" is removed from God in that realm, but
God can bridge this space and bring him back into the world.
Hence the cry for help as the turn to faith.

The poet in Psalm 42 initially uses totally different
imagery, although he later also picks up that flood metaphor (v
7). His initial image, however, stays entirely within the realm of
normal experience.

> As a hart longs
>   for flowing streams,
> so longs my soul
>   for thee, O God.
> My soul thirsts for God,
>   for the living God.
> When shall I come and behold
>   the face of God?
> My tears have been my food
>   day and night,
> while men say to me continually,
>   'Where is your God?'
>   (vv 1-3)

The metaphorical leitmotif at the beginning of the psalm is
"thirst," though this does not, of course, mean the normal thirst
on warm days; it is a life-threatening thirst such as that
experienced by someone lost in the desert. The poet portrays it
with the hart thirsting for water; it symbolizes his thirsting soul
in an image (that does not mean "immortal soul," but rather his

vital power, his living essence). So *far* from the life-giving water and yearning tensely for it, that is the soul in its relationship to God as the source of life; it *thirsts* for God (v 2). This thirst in the image thus designates the life-threatening remoteness of God that the person is suffering, but also represents that turn to faith which tensely reaches out for God. The poet lets the others, the world hostile to the sufferer, speak the words that God is absent: Where is your God? (v 3). The poet cannot and does not intend to argue that at all, but the spiteful question of those others presupposes that God's absence will continue. Of course, this quote is a fiction, placed into the mouth of the opposition by the supplicant himself (this is poetry, not a biographical text, and the hostile question is common turn of phrase). But then we find that the supplicant has made a kind of claim with this. The opposition says "your God," and this enables the supplicant to reclaim Him as his God, the God standing on the side of the suffering and believing. We will shortly see more of this in another text, but first this psalm needs to be followed a bit farther because it shows us something peculiar.

God's remoteness is not to be overcome here primarily by God's turning again to man. A movement on man's part is rather to be made possible, which will lead him to God. "When shall I . . . behold the face of God?"—that is, When will I come to the holy place?—thus verse 2. This is clearly articulated as a request in the continuation of this prayer of lament in Psalm 43:3 ff.

> Oh send out thy light and thy truth;
>   let them lead me,
> let them bring me to thy holy hill
>   and to thy dwelling! . . .
> and I will praise thee . . .
>   O God, my God.

Faith thus does not expect a mystical communion with God, and it does not even first mention the particular saving deed the supplicant's needs. Faith seeks rather his actual participation in the cult. Whenever he comes to the temple and the worship service he is close to Yahweh as the source of life. We should not underestimate this specific realism of God's presence, since it is not just a matter of some locale as the symbol of divine presence; this place is simultaneously the realm of the assembled congregation celebrating the worship service.

This certainly does not suppress the supplicant's rescue, but it is requested in a way that places it in a larger context. This becomes clear if we circumscribe the cited request for aid in prose. What are we to make of that "light" and "truth" that Yahweh is to send as guides? Of course, in prose we would say: Send me salvation and aid; "light" is a common and widely disturbed metaphor for salvation. Then, says the supplicant, I will praise you at the holy place in the middle of the celebrating congregation. But such prose does not really render the meaning correctly, since in the poetic metaphor it can be formulated precisely as only *one* procedure. That light-salvation is to illuminate his way to praise at Yahweh's holy place, or more precisely—as we read farther—at Yahweh's altar, since sacrifice and praise belong together according to tradition. That poetically unified formulation is the only correct one, since "life" and "praise of God" are one and the same for faith. Whoever received life from God belongs to the community of those who praise—or he rejoins them.

The text describes the expectation of faith in need, its future in which the "nearness of God" is experienced within the celebrating community. At the conclusion of this section let us describe his presence more closely with the beginning of Psalm 22. The supplicant begins:

My God, my God, why has thou forsaken me?
 Why art thou so far from helping me, from the words of my
  groaning?

We initially see characteristics already familiar to us: that remoteness is only potentially related to the lament here; the remote God does not hear. A similar, though rare turn of phrase is found in that lamenting question: you have forsaken me. One normally finds this kind of thing in the request: do not forsake me (eg, in Ps. 38:22). We encounter this "abandonment by God" as a motif in the lament of the individual only in this passage (and once more in the people's lament in Lam. 5:20 and as a lament of Zion in Isa. 49:14). But this phrase is no doubt more radical than the complaint about God's remoteness, since here one is reflecting the fact that God has turned away from this supplicant. The third element, however, is the most important part of this lament offering. The supplicant doggedly holds to the address "my God." He holds fast to the God who does not hear him and has forsaken him. This is where we find that movement of belief in the face of the easy possibility of unbelief in which one follows the words "curse God, and die." This also, however, preserves something rooted in man's past that supports one through this abandonment by God (cf vv 9 ff). This is more clearly articulated in the statements of trust. A moment of lasting relationship stands here over against that "remoteness." This turning of faith from godlessness to God found its most extreme expression in the Old Testament in the book of Job, who accuses and calls forth God against God in this legal struggle:

> My eye pours out tears to God,
> that he would maintain the right of a man with God.
> (Job 16:20*b* ff)

2. Lament and Trust

What is only alluded to in the address "my God" comes to full expression in the statements of trust: in the psalms they are in the strict sense the language of faith. At the beginning we spoke about the intensity and density of the language of the psalms which enables them to speak directly to men even today. In the scope of their experience of suffering they are well-suited for becoming the language of those who suffer in silence during all the ages, but they are more than that. Mankind's eternal lament can be found in many and various texts, and we find moving paradigms of lament everywhere in poetry, including laments in which the sufferer is able to express himself. The psalms' uniqueness lies in the fact that they are goal-oriented laments; they are not directed to just any higher being or to one's own encouragement, one's own spiritual uplifting, but rather to the God of Israel. This was manifested in the turn from (possible) unbelief to belief and in the call to the remote and yet near God. (NB: The spatial categories, as one can easily see in this example, are to be understood qualitatively, and this is also the case in the statement that God sits in heaven—possible ancient concepts notwithstanding. But this God who sits on a throne in heaven is also on earth, here in the temple; it is not the old view of the world which is naive, but rather only our customary image of it.) This directedness of the lament of God comes to total expression in the statements of trust, and for this reason the clear language of faith appears in them. Now some examples of this.

The most simple and common form is the simple assurance: "I trust in thee," or "I trust in thy steadfast love," or similar phrases (Ps. 25:2; 13:6; and elsewhere).[27] However, what is coming to expression here in this simple term (Hebrew *batah*) can appear in extremely plastic turns of phrase in which trust imagery becomes concrete and visible. A whole group of such phrases is associated with the asylum-function of the consecrated place.[28] The idea of the consecrated place as an asylum in which a person is protected from being pursued—because the deity takes him under protection—is very common; in the Old Testament it appears particularly as the place where the person who has killed (not the murderer) can seek refuge from revenge (Exod. 21:13 ff and elsewhere), but in real life it was probably beyond that a place of refuge for all kinds of people in need. This institution of the asylum has now been taken over into the language of the Psalms. The origin of this usage no doubt lies in the actual use of the asylum, though it was very soon severed from it and used metaphorically (without one always being able to make this distinction clearly in the individual texts). The frequent phrase "I protect myself in thee, I seek refuge in thee" (Heb. *ḥasah*) already belongs in this context, and the (linguistically alleged or actual) context of being pursued is often still discernible here, as for example in Psalm 7:1:

> O Lord my God, in thee do I take refuge;
> Save me from all my pursuers, and deliver me.

This same sense is carried in the phrase "thou art/Yahweh is my/our refuge" (Heb. *maḥasäh,* from the same root word, eg, Ps. 71:7). This is really the place of refuge, as the general use of the word still shows (eg, Ps. 104:18; "the rocks are a refuge for the badgers"), though here, too, it becomes partially clear, as Psalm 61:4 suggests: "For thou art my refuge, a strong tower against the enemy." If here the image of the fortified cities (as places of refuge for the rural population) is brought into the descriptive language, then this reference to the consecrated temple as a place of asylum becomes even more clearly articulated in the beautiful language imagery of the lament and trust psalms; this is how it appears in Psalm 57:1:

> Be merciful to me, O God, be merciful to me,
> for in thee my soul takes refuge;
> in the *shadow of thy wings* I will take refuge,
> till the storms of destruction pass by.

The image is again referring to something real, in this case to a peculiarity of the Jerusalem Temple. Yahweh's ark (the so-called Ark of the Covenant) stands in the Holy of Holies as a sign of Yahweh's presence, and arching over it are the wings of the cherubim on either side. Such cultic references color this imagery, which naturally cannot be analyzed logically (it then becomes distorted—one would already have difficulties with "your wings"), but must rather be seen in the power collecting together the various aspects and speaking to a deeper level. We can only mention some of its characteristics. We find in any case the reference to the particular place which owes its uniqueness to the presence of God. The "shadows of thy wings" is there as the protection granted by the present God and which initially covers the entire consecrated area (if one is thinking of the actual granting of asylum). This is, however, now taken up in general—although above and beyond as well—by the believing trust that makes use of this language. One can, by the way, make even more associations in this imagery. Even the word "shadow" has a particular association in a hot, shadowless country, and the "wings" may well simultaneously evoke the image of the bird hovering above its young (Deut. 32:11a; Isa. 31:5 might also be compared here). The image does not become imprecise because of such different references, but rather gains in significance.

Another group of statements of trust speaks of Yahweh as the supplicant's "portion" ("The Lord is my chosen portion" Ps. 16:5; 142:5 and elsewhere). This formulation is also based on actual custom. During the parceling of a community's (newly acquired) farmland the Levite priest did not receive a portion, but rather "Yahweh is his portion." The straight realistic meaning is, he lives off the sacrificial offerings and consecrated gifts brought to Yahweh. In the psalms, however, this very quickly acquired a figurative meaning, and refers to the general dependence of the supplicant's existence on the God who gives life and support. This believing trust expresses itself in yet another way in the common phrase, "Yahweh, my rock," and in similar ones (Ps. 18:2; 19:14; and elsewhere). This, too, refers to different things. First we find the reference to an actual part of the Jerusalem Temple: the holy rock on which the Holy of Holies allegedly sits along with the ark (according to other versions, the altar). Yahweh, of course, "is" not the rock, nor is he bound to it, but what it means to the supplicant can be expressed by the metaphor taken from the reference system of the present God. The "rock" is then simultaneously the basis, the place threatening to be lost by the supplicant—we may think here of his plunge into the chaos floods, a plunge out of the world (see above p 49). We then find the images of the secured fortress and high place of refuge that need no commentary.

These and similar phrases in which trust is articulated appear in the middle of laments, and are actually their supporting framework. The motif of trust, however, can also appear in psalms of praise and has even acquired a certain independence in some texts. We will now take a brief look at one of these.

> The Lord is my shepherd, I shall not want;
>   he makes me lie down in green pastures.
> He leads me beside still waters;
>   he restores my soul.
> He leads me in paths of righteousness
>   for his name's sake.
> Even though I walk through the valley of the
> shadow of death,
>   I fear no evil;
> for thou art with me;
>   thy rod and thy staff,
>   they comfort me.
>
> Thou preparest a table before me
>   in the presence of my enemies;
> thou anointest my head with oil,
>   my cup overflows.
> Surely goodness and mercy shall follow me
>   all the days of my life;

and I shall dwell in the house of the Lord
   for ever.

(Ps. 23)

This well-known psalm juxtaposes two images, that of Yahweh as the protecting shepherd and as the divine host. One should not—as often happens—misunderstand the shepherd image as an idyll; this becomes immediately clear if one imagines the actual life circumstances of oriental shepherds and herds, with the threat of scarce water, sparse pasture, wild animals, and robbers. The image was originally used to refer to Yahweh's relationship to Israel (Ps. 80:1; the shepherd does, of course, lead the flock), though here the relation is appropriated by the individual: Yahweh leads him on a righteous ("saving") path, and he places his honor ("for his name's sake"!) in taking up and accepting the individual. This text, too, speaks of the danger that faith can encounter. The path through the dark valley represents this, just as in the second part the enemy does. But now faith does not say then, "you are remote," but rather, "for thou art with me."

   Yes, this is certainly a different situation, and the danger has not yet become that extreme threat out of which the cry of lament issues. The supplicant can still confess, "I fear no evil"—but he *has* already encountered evil. Nonetheless we have to notice that danger and God's nearness merge together when God accompanies one through the dark valley; ultimately we find extremely old experiences of Israel's nomadic ancestors preserved here. Above all, however, this is a formulation of what renders possible the believer's cry of lament in the time of need, and a formulation of what he can recall even when he is lamenting God's remoteness.

   This image of the "path," which appears here along with that of the shepherd, is so common that it does not seem strange even today; the image of the divine host, however, is less familiar. The realistic idea of the maintenance of temple personnel—or perhaps of someone seeking asylum—probably also stood behind these images originally, but again this has long since been generalized and now expresses the confidence that even in the face of the enemy God will abundantly grant what the supplicant needs for life. The "enemies" as the signature of need are not overlooked, but "only goodness and mercy shall *pursue* me" (as one would have to translate it literally). The danger is already suspended by the God who grants a reprieve and accompanies man further.

This is how faith expresses it, a faith that is *certain* of such divine aid precisely because it experiences that aid, but which at the same time also takes note of the imminent threat or possible danger. And this certainty remains in effect even after the moment of experienced salvation; it does not always need a direct confirmation in order for that trust to be preserved in the absence of immediate experience of salvation. Ancient Israel's texts demonstrate a certain sober realism here; they do not always speak about faith in extreme situations, but rather first about the normal fluctuation between untroubled life and possible danger in which one can nonetheless remain without fear. Israel did, however, admittedly also have to speak about the extreme situations. We have seen how it did this using the model of the ancestor Abraham (see above, pp 31 ff). There faith was expected to concentrate on the God who had defined himself through the promise, and to differentiate between the perpetually valid promise and what was seemingly its only possible realization. Another extreme situation is one's own death, particularly premature death. Someone threatened by a premature death naturally expects to be rescued and is allowed to expect it. But the other question poses itself just as naturally. What am I left with if there is no rescue?

Ancient Israel offered various answers to this question. One answer proved ultimately to be insufficient: that it will go well with the pious and badly with the godless. The answer was not totally false, but held true only in a very limited fashion and was in any case no externally applicable standard. The answer of Old Testament faith is articulated in a well-known section of Psalm 73.

That psalm begins again with the problem that was already old when the psalm was composed: the good fortune of the godless. Their fortune as well as their godlessness are portrayed in an almost exemplary manner (vv 4-12); they, too, proceed on the presumption that God does not take note of what happens on earth (see above p 46). In contrast we see the supplicant's own fate.

> All in vain have I kept my heart clean
> and washed my hands in innocence.
> For all day long I have been stricken,
> and chastened every morning.
> (vv 13 ff)

This supplicant, too, must reject the temptation of unbelief (v 15), but he does not *understand*, and that is part of his distress (v 16). The answer to this tormenting question surprises him when it comes, and it is not just an irrational answer. It is comprehensible, and for this reason the poet admits afterward that he was foolish and stupid in his bitterness (vv 21 ff). The solution to the problem occurs to him when he views the end, first the end of the godless.

> Truly thou dost set them in slippery
> places;
> thou dost make them fall to ruin.
> How they are destroyed in a moment,
> swept away utterly by terrors!
> (vv 18 ff)

This initially appears to be only the extension of the old expectation. Even if the distribution of fortune and misfortune to the pious and godless be reversed for awhile, one must expect that in the end the righteous world order will be reestablished. But this answer, which is considered in the Old Testament, remains behind the answer given to the supplicant in this psalm, because just as he has learned to understand the end of the godless, so also must he now learn to understand his own end.

> Nevertheless I am continually with thee;
>   thou dost hold my right hand.
> Thou dost guide me with thy counsel,
>   and afterward thou wilt receive me to glory.
> Whom have I in heaven but thee?
>   And there is nothing upon earth that I desire besides thee.
> My flesh and my heart may fail,
>   but God is the strength of my heart and my portion for
>   ever.
>
>   (vv 23-26)

Martin Luther translated the beginning of verse 23 (to the effect): "Nevertheless I remain always with thee," and from this we get the phrase about the "nevertheless of faith." The word "nevertheless" admittedly does not stand in the text, and even if it can, on the one hand, articulate how far faith extends, it can also give rise to misunderstanding, as if what is meant here is the believer's courageous, defiant posture. It is, however, faith's sudden insight, a total certainty that is granted and then results also in a certain behavior—though perhaps more a passivity than defiant resistance. That "nevertheless" is admittedly valid, even in the face of appearances and of the believer's worldly experience; not in every case, because he also experiences inner-worldly rescue, but it holds above and beyond that in extreme situations. This radical certainty of faith thus does not mean that nothing happens in the physical worldly sense, though faith can nonetheless elevate itself above the unpleasantries. It means rather that a saving takes place even contrary to all appearances, even when with death one is seemingly encountering only misfortune. In this way faith acquires the largest possible room for play.

Compared with this kind of end in splendor, the end of the godless is an end with terror, and this difference has a very simple reasoning behind it. The supplicant can base his confident expectation on nothing more than the certainty of a lasting communion with God which extends beyond all misfortune. He expresses this clearly with the common turn of phrase already discussed: Yahweh is "his portion," that is to say: God provides for his life—even when it is ended. Yahweh was not the portion of the godless.

One can only allude to how this saving act is concretized on the basis of an ongoing communion with God, since it is, as it were, God's business. The supplicant uses an expression here that perhaps reflects an old concept. One hears, for example, that Yahweh took up Elisha into heaven. This kind of thing might lie behind the phrase "thou wilt receive me to glory." This is not, however, certain, and the supplicant very likely did not expect this kind of exceptional occurrence. It remains an image, and all that is important is the qualification of the certain future with God. That is what is meant by "glory." The uniqueness of faith's expression here is that it cannot refer back to similar saving experiences in the past, but rather only to the God whose proximity has always meant shelter and life and who will always be there in death. The knowledge "I am always with thee" is enough, and it is the counterpoint to the cry of lament "Why art thou so far?" Both statements, however, are mutually determinative, since that lament, too, is only possible against the background of trust. In the Old Testament it is admittedly the exception to hear that God is also near in the most extreme danger and that objectively there is no more abandonment by God or remoteness associated with God during suffering. This becomes the rule in New Testament faith, which sees God present in the death of Jesus. However, the texts which speak of God's remoteness have not just become meaningless because of this, since abandonment by God becomes very much the experiential form of the most extreme fear, both subjectively and during temptation, and that transition from unbelief to belief has always remained relevant.

In all this we have encountered and conjured up the language of only a selection of the rich texts concerned with trust. But what have we gained except the knowledge that at that time people expressed their laments as well as their trust with such words? In any case we have the reference to the texts as the language school of faith. They do not just teach the suffering person how to lament, since the poet is also able to do this: "And though man is struck with silence in his torment, a god gave me the words to express what I suffer."[29] In these texts in which lament emerges from trust, the person who is speechless, not only in suffering, but above all before God, can find his language and speech again.

3. Lament and Praise

The discussion of faith in Israel's laments would be incomplete without a look at the relationship between lament and praise, so we will now, in conclusion, speak briefly about this. The lament, and with it faith in need, assigns to man a place between praise and praise: he looks back at the past praise of God (as faith's past) and expects a future praising of God (on the basis of the saving acts as the future of faith). In this double reference we once again see more clearly that faith as a kind of behavior (or a posture) also has a content. These psalms of praise show how that God to whom faith flees in need has given himself to Israel as an experience, and thus Israel's songs of praise are also expressions of its faith. One finds this confirmed already in Israel's oldest song of praise; a small hymn (Exod. 15:21; the previous, thorough version is later) appears as an addendum to the story of the Red Sea miracle, whose end had spoken about Israel's faith (see above pp 35 ff):

> Sing to the Lord, for he has triumphed gloriously;
> the horse and his rider he has thrown into the sea.

Here it is a matter of a single act in history; other themes are added in the songs of praise in the Book of Psalms, above all the praise of the God of creation who maintains the world. If we call such songs of praise expressions of faith, then we must also admittedly remain aware of the possible modern reactions to this. First, there are those for whom "faith" only conceals an insecurity in knowing. But faith and intellectual knowledge are not really competitors here, and at any rate, faith involves a higher measure of certainty, not a lower one. Neither does that mildly grumbling reaction belong here which complains variously that the world in reality is not whole, and is not kept by God, and that the songs of praise only see the world in a kind of transfigured light. We really have to realize that ancient Israel's experiences of suffering were by no means less intense than such experiences today; Israel often enough personally experienced starvation, epidemics, earthquakes, and wars of destruction that were cruelly carried out against them. But it knew how to differentiate between the times of praise and the times of lament, and it thus knew about praise from the depths of suffering, but did not indulge in lament during a period of true good fortune.

We cannot speak further here about Israel's independent songs of praise, since portraying the content of faith in this way would require an entire theology of the Old Testament. We will limit our discussion to the relationship between lament and praise in two texts in which this relationship is expressed and clarified. Then we will briefly discuss the expectation of future praise, since we already encountered this in psalms 42 and 43. There the request was formulated in a way viewing rescue and praise as one event. The locus of this reference to the future in the lament is normally the vow of praise, often articulated at the end of a prayer of lament. The supplicant vows to offer public praise in the temple after Yahweh has rescued him, which means he will then tell about what happened to him and how he was rescued. Even more important in our own context is the lament's reference to past praise, and we will first look at this in a communal lament.

> Give ear, O Shepherd of Israel,
>   thou who leadest Joseph like a flock!
> Thou who art enthroned upon the cherubim, shine forth
>   before Ephraim and Benjamin and Manasseh!
> Stir up thy might,
>   and come to save us! . . .
>
> Thou didst bring a vine out of Egypt;
>   thou didst drive out the nations and plant it.
> Thou didst clear the ground for it;
>   it took deep root and filled the land. . . .
> it sent out its branches to the sea,
>   and its shoots to the River.
>
> (Ps. 80:1-2; 8-9; 11)

The final verses cited offer an extremely transparent image of the Exodus and acquisition of the land; taken in and for itself that could be part of a hymn. Here, however, it is an element in a communal-lament psalm; what is it doing in this context? The answer is simple. It wants, of course, to move Yahweh to come to the aid of his people once again, to remind him not to give up the work he began long ago. This "word in God's ear," however, is only one side of the story. That which is told in reference to earlier good fortune is now itself the basis of faith and renders the lament possible, since that lament would be meaningless and only a miserable crying out to an empty heaven if it were not *certain* about what the presently lamenting community were referring to out of its previous times of praise.

Our second example will show how the individual can also use this reference. Let us look at a section of Psalm 22, whose introductory verses were already discussed (see above p 52).

> Yet thou art holy,
>   enthroned on the praises of Israel.
> In thee our fathers trusted;
>   they trusted, and thou didst deliver them.
> To thee they cried, and were saved;
>   in thee they trusted, and were not disappointed.
> But I am a worm, and no man;
>   scorned by men, and despised by the people.
> All who see me mock at me . . .
> He committed his cause to the Lord; let him deliver him,
>   let him rescue him, for he delights in him!
>
> Yet thou art he who took me from the womb;
>   thou didst keep me safe upon my mother's breast.
> Upon thee was I cast from my birth,
>   and since my mother bore me thou hast been my God.
> Be not far from me,
>   for trouble is near
>   and there is none to help.
>
> (vv 3-11)

The first and last parts of the section cited are expressions of trust, but to what is the supplicant—abandoned by God—referring (v 1)? He explains why he nonetheless can still say "my God" by referring to his own past history with that God, a history that began at his birth. "Thou brought me into the world" is also a statement of the praise by the individual. In the first section, however, the supplicant refers to Israel's praise. God reigns as the Holy One in the temple, praised by Israel's hymns, hymns praising the God who maintains and preserves the world. The supplicant has fallen away from this world, he is "no longer a man" (v 7) and does not participate in Israel's praise. He refers to them, however, because the countless saving experiences of the fathers are collected there. They cried out and were rescued, and thus a suffering person can cry out anew. His faith expresses itself in the fact that he holds up to *his* God past experience—his own, and now also Israel's—because that is part of it. Faith does not call upon just any God for help, but rather only upon the one, familiar God of Israel confessed in praise. People contemporaneous with Israel also knew of a supplicant's relationship to a personal God,[30] but hardly of the same exclusivity of lament.

The believer expects help and rescue from his God and can expect it; but have we not fallen back behind precisely what the poet in Psalm 73 became sure of? He does not exclude the possibility of secular rescue either. If faith wanted to do without this, it would push the effectiveness of its God to the periphery of its world, and would "believe" only in a God of emergencies and extreme situations. That is not biblical faith. That must think its subject through—all the way to the extreme—but whenever it refers to general praise of God, it sees God at work precisely in all of reality. A later word of this people so versed in suffering may clarify, here at the end in view of all these examples, just how things stand with Israel's expectations of deliverance. It tells of the three boys who refuse to worship the foreign cultic image as ordered and are thus to be thrown into the fiery oven. The king asks them, "Who would the God be who could rescue you from my hand?" And they answer, "If it be so, our God whom we serve is able to deliver us from the burning fiery furnace; and he will deliver us out of your hand, O king. But if not, be it known to you, O king, that we will not serve your gods . . . " (Dan. 3:15, 17-18). The deliverance is God's, and there is no reason to deny this God.

III. The Faith of the Prophets

Israel's prophets are represented here only by two of their greatest figures, Isaiah (eighth century B.C.) and Deutero-Isaiah (sixth century B.C.). This can be justified because for the one, Isaiah, the faith Israel withholds becomes a main theme, and eventually the reason for the coming judgment of Yahweh. For the other, the second, unknown prophet of the Exile, whose voice we hear in Isaiah 40–55, faith is an elementary part of God's inbreaking, final salvation, though not as a presupposition of that salvation. Deutero-Isaiah is thus of special significance because he formulates theological insights which, although they do not simply take over the New Testament proclamation of faith, can nonetheless merge with that proclamation.

The contribution of other Old Testament prophets to the theme of faith can be mentioned here only in passing. One should not at any rate assume they all wanted to make such a contribution. A prophet as significant as Amos speaks only of Israel's coming demise and end; in view of this end faith is hardly a question. Neither can believing the prophet's message change anything in that future already determined by Yahweh. "Perhaps"—this is the best that can be said, and is likely part of a somewhat later redaction of the Book of Amos—perhaps Yahweh will be merciful if you strive for the good instead of evil (Amos 5:14-15). The prophet himself can say, "For thus says the Lord to the house of Israel: 'Seek me and live' " (5:4). But the main theme remains, "The end has come upon my people Israel" (8:2). We see: Israel's relationship to God is taken up, if at all, under a different aspect than that of faith.

On the other hand, one can find numerous examples of errant faith and false trust, not only in Amos (eg, 5:5; or 5:18-20:

the passage about the day of Yahweh yearned for so strongly, which will be "darkness" instead of "light"), but also in Micah. The prophet counts the crimes of the Jerusalem upper class and then continues, "Yet they lean upon the Lord and say, 'Is not the Lord in the midst of us? No evil shall come upon us' " (3:11). That is a statement of faith, just as pious supplicants in the psalms were able to speak it since the beginning, in the same way the congregation expresses its trust (cf eg, Ps. 46:6). But in the face of the evil deeds it proves to be a lie. Above all Jeremiah should be mentioned in this context. His dispute with the false prophets peaks in the accusation that they "strengthen the hands of the evil-doers." That is, their proclamation of salvation strengthens the blasphemers in their deeds by awakening confidence where penitence should be found (Jer. 23:14, 17). Jeremiah's temple speech (Jer. 7) is, however, the most well-known. The prophet calls the word of trust—"This is the temple of the Lord" (ie, "Yahweh is present here and grants protection")—a word of deception which one should not trust, since again it is the evil deeds that turn such faith into a farce. "And then you come and stand before me in this house . . . and say, 'we are delivered!'—only to go on doing all these abominations? Has this house, which is called by my name, become a den of robbers in your eyes?" This is what the prophet must proclaim in the name of Yahweh (Jer. 7:10 ff). One cannot really suppose Jeremiah's contemporaries relied in conscious cynicism on Yahweh's protection and at the same time broke his commandments; subjectively their faith probably appeared genuine. But the prophets brings the factual discrepancy to light. Faith without obedience, or a religiosity which still allows life in the community to degenerate, is a lie; indeed, one is deceiving oneself because such trust is without support.

The essence of faith is also clarified with this kind of negative example. In the final analysis, however, it is a matter of the simple insight that a relationship of trust between God and man—just as one between man and man—cannot be partially

sustained and partially cheated. Isaiah and Deutero-Isaiah are
also concerned with a deficiency in faith, but what is expected as
faith is ultimately more instructive than its misuse. In the
following discussion, the faith of the prophets is also their own
faith, but it is always more than their private affair. Their faith
concerns for the most part something universal—Israel's
relationship to God in which the prophets participate, or of which
they take cognizance, in a representative fashion for the
recalcitrant Israel. But this comes out quite differently in the two
prophets, and we will now examine each of them individually.

(A.) ISAIAH

The prophet belongs in the last third of the eighth century
B.C. The message he had to deliver accompanied both the fall of
the Northern Kingdom, Israel (722) as well as the difficult
disputes in which the Southern Kingdom, Judah, saw itself
involved. These were the years in which the Neo-Assyrian
empire under Tiglath Pileser III and his successors attained its
zenith. His power expanded the empire at large by means of
military campaigns, which soon included the states of Syria and
Palestine. The people, however, made every effort to resist the
Assyrian threat or throw off the Assyrian yoke. The high-level
politics of defense alliance and commitments as well as military
armament are the main themes of the age, and the prophet's
word about faith goes out into these turbulent decades. Initially
it is a message bound to a certain situation, but it then points
beyond its own time when it was preserved and transmitted.

1. Faith at the Time of the Syro-Ephraimite War

a. Isaiah 7: Yahweh and the King

The particular events of the year 733 B.C. can be quickly
recounted. The Aramaen kingdom of Damascus (the "Syrians")

allied itself with Northern Israel ("Ephraim") against Asher; Judah is also to participate in the coalition, and when its king, Ahaz, refuses, it is to be coerced with military force. The result of the undertaking—Ahaz is calling the Assyrains to help and thus forcing the allies to withdraw from his country—is still quite open when Isaiah is sent to the king with a message we now read about in Isaiah 7. The prophet is supposed to seek out the king just when he is inspecting the city's water supply (the vulnerable point during a siege) and say to him:

> Take heed, be quiet, do not fear, and do not let your heart be faint because of these two smoldering stumps of fire-brands. . . . Because Syria, with Ephraim and the son of Remaliah, has devised evil against you. . . . Thus says the Lord God: It shall not stand, and it shall not come to pass. For the head of Syria is Damascus, and the head of Damascus is Rezin. . . . And the head of Ephraim is Samaria, and the head of Samaria is the son of Remaliah. If you will not believe, surely you shall not be established.[31]
>
> (vv 4-9)

The final sentence reads in effect as follows in the Luther-translation, "If you do not believe, you will not remain," and this is better to the extent that the word-play of the original text is imitated. "To believe" and "to remain" stand in a very close relationship. But what does "believe" mean here? Since we are concerned here with a passage that is crucially important for Old Testament faith, we should take a closer look at the structure of the prophet's words here. It begins with an admonition (v 4) and ends with a warning (v 9b), each apparently related to the other. Between them stands an unconditional judgment against the enemies that, as is frequently the case in this figure of speech, names both their guilt and their fate. The kingdoms of Damascus and (Northern) Israel will no longer exist; this has been announced by Yahweh and is unconditionally valid, whether the person to whom the passage is addressed, the king, believes it or not. And yet his faith is questioned because continuance of his kingdom depends on it. No doubt his future is also at stake here, though not because of the hostile attack, since the coalition's threat is innocuous. What would a believing king have to do? The word of admonition at the beginning tells us. "Be quiet, do not fear, and take seriously the fact that there is no reason at all for fear" (in symbolic form, "It is only the smoldering remains of a burned-out fire"). Faith thus requires fearlessness, though not universally, and also not just foolish courage. The word play, the compelling relationship between "believing" and "remaining," is to be taken seriously here. The prophet's statement reminds the listener that Yahweh promised the Davidic dynasty perpetual duration (through the prophecy of Nathan, 2 Sam. 7). The duration of the Davidic dynasty rests solely on this promise, and Yahweh has now actualized this guarantee in the word of destruction spoken over the enemies (who want to destroy the Davidic dynasty). The word play then says that faith is only the reverse side of the same thing, and not the presupposition which is then to be followed by "remaining." It is now a matter of accepting this configuration and of basing the continuation of the dynasty totally on Yahweh's actualized promise. (Of course, just as with Abraham in Gen. 15, the king must "consider Yahweh's word to be true"; but this is by no means a theoretical affair—see above p 26.) That fearlessness in question here thus has a very firm basis, the basis on which the dynasty has always rested. But then one has to ask again What should the king actually do? This report of the prophet, written down later, no longer shows us any recognizable demands because the prophet wants to lead the scene to the decisive element, the relationship between God and king;[32] but we can presume with some certainty that there were concrete demands of some sort. Interpreters are admittedly not in agreement concerning their content. While some think King Ahaz was only to dispense with the request for aid from the

Assyrian king (by which he in fact subjugated himself to the Assyrians) and fearlessly go on with the defense preparations, others think the prophet demanded that the king dispense with all military activity. These appear to be historically inconsequential matters, but considering the significance of this text for the understanding of faith, there may just be something to it. What consequences does faith have here—the fearless cooperation in Yahweh's work to protect the city and the dynasty, or total passivity? In view of the transmitted texts this will hardly be possible to determine, but the analogy of Isaiah's proclamation of the end-time speaks emphatically for the second answer (above all cf Isa. 22:8-11). The order of the day was thus passivity, to let Yahweh act, not to stand in the way of his work and thus to forego any defense. However, we must not misunderstand this. First of all, this kind of concrete conclusion is not, of course, meant as a general course of action for all times. It is, however, a serious admonition to the faith of all ages to consider such concrete consequences, since they could be imposed anew. Above all, this passivity did not here mean the convenience of simply doing nothing. If the king was being commanded to omit doing what one knew full well was his natural duty, then this was an extremely difficult command and presupposed a decision that was highly questionable from the perspective of political pragmatism.

The king resisted this command and this decision, as the prophet reports in the highly dramatic scene which follows (Isa. 7:10-17). The prophet demands that the king ask for a sign from Yahweh, but the king withdraws from it all with a pious-sounding statement, "I will not put the Lord to the test." This is only apparent piousness, because with this he resists trust in Yahweh, and resists faith. This is also why Yahweh's judgment is spoken to him. Things stay the same concerning the fall of the two current enemy states, but in the final analysis Judah will meet the same fate. People have often speculated about what political consequences the king's faith would have had. Wasn't the commandment nothing more than utopian? Or did not the prophet himself really have the wider political perspective (since the Assyrians would have acted without having to be asked)? Isaiah did not himself see it this way, and the suspicion of utopianism misses the point. The decision against Yahweh was not made when the king was taking specific political measures, but rather long before, when he was not willing seriously to base the continuation of the Davidic dynasty on Yahweh's promise. That discrepancy between the holiday utterances of the old promise of Nathan and day-to-day political practice was only thrown into relief in this scene. In the face of a word of *salvation*, the decision between belief and unbelief was made publicly.

In our interpretation we have passed over the two signs mentioned in the scene. Already at the beginning there is the Isaiah-son with the name of misfortune, "only a remnant shall return (from the catastrophe)"; he gives the encounter the more weighty background. Yahweh's judgment on Judah has long been made, but he offers once more the chance for faith. Then there is the much-discussed and controversial sign of Immanuel, again a name with symbolic meaning. The meaning is simple if one can just see into the complex structure of the text. Here we find a sign of salvation within an utterance of condemnation, and the resolution of this apparent contradiction is easily found in a comparison with the previous text. There it was an utterance of salvation that brought up the crisis between belief and unbelief; now, after the decision for unbelief has been made, this constellation is secured once and for all. That sign of salvation—and the salvation event to which it points—becomes a sign of condemnation and an event of misfortune for the person who rejected it. This is even more easy to understand if one transposes it to the level of the expected event. The attack on Judah by the Aramaic-Israelite coalition will still fail, but this no longer has salvation significance for Judah and its king, since the same Assyrian who will destroy the coalition will also take over Judah.[33]

b. Isaiah 8: Yahweh and the People

In the scene in the previous chapter when the decision
about the future is seen to be totally dependent upon the king's
belief or unbelief, this need not seem strange since in the case of
a people of antiquity the king could represent the entire
people. This perspective on things is not unrealistic either,
since the decisions grounded in various mutual relationships of
a community—the everyday necessities as well as the goals and
wishes—appear in the final analysis in the plans and activities of
the heads of state. The prophet held fast in his own text—a text
speaking in its own way about reluctant faith—to the view that
the king's unbelief is not the personal weakness of an
individual, but rather represents the attitude of his age. Again
there is first a sign, the birth of a child with the peculiar name
"the spoil speeds, the prey hastes," that is, the fall and plunder
of the two enemy states will still be carried out by the Assyrians;
however—and the prophet continues:

> Because this people has refused the waters of Shiloah that
> flow gently, . . . therefore, behold, the Lord is bringing up
> against them the waters of the River, mighty and
> many, . . . it will rise over all its channels and go over all its
> banks; and it will sweep on into Judah, it will overflow and
> pass on, reaching even to the neck.
>
> (8:6-8)

This splendid image needs little commentary. The waters of the
(Euphrates) river are, of course, the wished-for Assyrians, but
now the water will "reach even to the neck." The misfortune is
in reality the fact that disbelief gets exactly what it wanted. The
refused waters of Shiloah were Jerusalem's own foundation of
existence, too undistinguished a one to have been capable of
establishing faith factually. But they pointed beyond to the God
who made faith possible and who could expect faith, and who

now put the world power into motion against his people. If this text referred only to the refused faith, what then remains for belief after unbelief becomes manifest and the calamity has been predetermined? The next text Isaiah composes in his small piece at the end of the Syrian-Ephraimite War leads a step farther.

> For the Lord spoke thus to me . . . and warned me not to walk in the way of this people, saying: "Do not call conspiracy all that this people call conspiracy, and do not fear what they fear, nor be in dread. But the Lord of hosts, him you shall regard as holy; let them be your fear, and let him be your dread. And he will become . . . a stone of offense, and a rock of stumbling to both houses of Israel, a trap and a snare to the inhabitants of Jerusalem."
>
> (8:11-14)

Can one still speak about faith here at all, and isn't fear and dread before Yahweh precisely its opposite? Certainly the term is not missing, but the text is clearly placed into a context in which faith is a question. The prophet must be warned by Yahweh to stay away from the way of unbelief, since that unbelief does not take Yahweh into consideration. Israel's belief, however, is also supposed to take Yahweh into consideration during misfortune and catastrophe. It is expected to see the deeper dimension of the secular, external events. That is, it is expected to see Yahweh at work even in judgment upon his own unbelieving people.

The immediately following text shows that such an interpretation is not simply plucked out of thin air, a text with which the prophet concludes his scroll from the year 733.

> Bind up the testimony, seal the teaching among my disciples. I will wait for the Lord, who is hiding his face from the house of Jacob, and I will hope in him. Behold, I and the children whom the Lord has given me are signs and portents in Israel from the Lord of hosts, who dwells on Mount Zion.
>
> (8:16-18)

The binding and sealing refer to the prophet's scroll, which is to be preserved as a legally valid document. But in view of the total calamity for Israel and Judah written on it, what does the prophet have left? Certainly not the hope that he and his small group of pupils will escape the general calamity, but rather only a hoping and waiting—that means waiting in tension, and with the greatest awareness—for the God who is now "hiding his face" and thus bringing on the catastrophe. This appears to be a paradox, but it is precisely the turn to faith we also encountered in the psalms. The only difference is that there a certain future was normally expected from this God, salvation or rescue from a particular danger. In Isaiah, however, one finds nothing of this future; there is only the misfortune and destruction the prophet had to announce in the face of unbelief. Thus only hope in God himself remains, the God who—as the prophet here can still say—dwells on Mount Zion, and who as the judging God nonetheless *remains* there and maintains a sign of his presence with Zion. The prophet is not able to say at the moment what this will mean concretely, that is God's matter; but faith reaches out of this future hidden with God on the other side, the faith waiting for the hidden God. It is here a matter of the future of the people of God, not specifically of Isaiah's own. However, what this means in the face of the end awaiting Israel is for God to know just as was the case concerning Abraham and the future of the promise, when he was supposed to sacrifice his son.

2. Faith at the Time of the Uprisings (before 711 and 701 B.C.)

We are now inquiring about faith during a certain time and under certain political conditions. This is possible in the case of Isaiah because faith is demanded here in a recognizable historical situation. Nonetheless this is not, of course, merely a matter of a historical-past faith, but rather of the question of how faith is realized and brought to expression under different historical conditions.

Isaiah's proclamation reaches across a time span of three-and-a-half decades, up to the end of the century, and one is already surprised that after the proclamation of 733 there was any continuation at all. The predicted end of all Israel had not yet come, and even when in the year 722, the Northern Kingdom ended once and for all, Judah continued on as a dependent kingdom. What is then to be said about the fulfillment of prophetic statements concerning the future? Attempts have been made to interpret Isaiah 8:17 from the perspective of this question. The prophet is supposedly hoping and waiting for the advent of the divine judgment. But this is not very likely in the first place because the prophet is nowhere really mindful of his reputation as a "clairvoyant" and because this would in any case be a misunderstanding of the prophetic office. *He* wasn't responsible for the future, God was, and God remained free to structure what was coming according to his own conception—*that* is how the prophet saw it. He did not have to be concerned about how the divine statement concerning the future would be realized. Isaiah gives the most impressive example for this in one of his final statements. If until 701 he had announced the preservation of Zion in the midst of the catastrophe, then he must now—after Jerusalem and Zion really had been spared the final Assyrian attack—speak a new word. The judgment will go farther, all the way to the bitter end, and the city with its hill of Zion will become a sterile field forever, a joy of wild asses and one of the many wasted hills upon which the shepherd drives his flocks (32:13 ff). That, however, is already the end of Judah's history at the time of Isaiah. Previous to this was the epoch of the great uprisings in which the Judean king, Hezekiah, more (701) or less (711) had a part, and which in these years had already been put down by the Assyrians. What is Isaiah's role during this period, and how does faith come to expression here? Just as in the beginning, in the year 733, it is a political statement. We can clarify this quickly by considering a few situations in which the prophet becomes politically involved. Emissaries from the Ethiopian king, who had just conquered Egypt, come to negotiate an anti-Assyrian alliance. But Isaiah sends them away; the God who is now waiting in infinite quietness will proceed *alone* (ch 18). At another time emissaries from Philistia appear in order to condemn the uprising; Isaiah gives them a statement of catastrophe to take along and the answer, "The Lord has founded Zion"—that has always been the single, totally adequate protection (14:28-32). The prophet does not get in the way of his people's quest for freedom, but he points out to them that the people of God can seek freedom and protection only from Yahweh. Thus there is a cry of woe to those who in the strict sense pursue godless politics.

> Woe to the rebellious children, says the Lord,
>   who carry out a plan, but not mine;
> and who make a league, but not of my spirit,
>   that they may add sin to sin;
> who set out to go down to Egypt,
>   without asking for my counsel,
> to take refuge in the protection of Pharaoh
>   and to seek shelter in the shadow of Egypt.
>   (30:1-2)

The prophet employs the language of the psalms: to take refuge, to seek shelter in the shadow. That was the language of faith that turned to Yahweh, and it is taken up here to throw into relief the practical behavior of unbelief. A second example is quite similar.

> Woe to those who go down to Egypt for help
>   and rely on horses,
> who trust in chariots because they are many
>   and in horsemen . . .

but do not look to the Holy One of Israel
　or consult the Lord.
And yet he is wise and brings disaster . . . .
The Egyptians are men, and not God;
　and their horses are flesh, and not spirit.
When the Lord stretches out his hand,
　the helper will stumble, and he who is helped will fall,
　and they will all perish together.

(31:1-3)

Here, too, we can make do with very few comments. Horses and chariots were the most important weapons of war in the Ancient Orient from about the middle of the second millenium B.C., and they represent modern weaponry in general. The contrast "flesh" (mortal) and "spirit" alludes to a certain tradition and becomes comprehensible within that context. The tradition of Yahweh's wars reports that since the beginning Yahweh himself has conducted Israel's wars, and that he has bestowed the spirit upon the human leaders of the Israelite armies, a spirit enabling them to perform extraordinary deeds. This tradition is radicalized here[34] in order to bring that element to expression upon which Israel's security now rests. God acts, not man; again this is for Isaiah the one, decisive statement of faith. In the face of a popular modern misunderstanding we must, however, add, things are occurring here quite "naturally." The prophet knows, for example, that Judah and its Egyptian allies will be defeated by the Assyrians, but what does it matter, since Assyria, too, will come under the divine judgment. The only thing significant in all this, as far as the prophet is concerned, is the fact that Yahweh is acting, and for this reason he can take this fundamental view to the extreme: "And the Assyrian shall fall by a sword, not of man" (31:8). Did it not fall to the Babylonians and Medes (although 100 years later)? The prophet would have been satisfied and would not have had to retract his statement.

　There is specific talk of faith in Isaiah's later period, once

more in a saying in which the prophet portrays the complexity
of the future relationship between belief and unbelief.

> Therefore hear the word of the Lord, you scoffers . . .
> Because you have said, "We have made a covenant with
>   death . . .
> when the overwhelming scourge passes through
>   it will not come to us;
> for we have made lies our refuge,
>   and in falsehood we have taken shelter";
> therefore thus says the Lord God,
> "Behold, I am laying in Zion for a foundation
>   a stone, a tested stone,
> a precious cornerstone, of a sure foundation:
>   'He who believes will not be in haste.'
> And I will make justice the line,
>   and righteousness the plummet;
> and hail will sweep away the refuge of lies,
>   and waters will overwhelm the shelter."
>
> (28:14-17)

This saying is particularly difficult for us to understand because
the imagery is not familiar and because it reflects once more the
connection between the work of divine salvation and divine
judgment. The point of contention is again foreign policy,
specifically the alliance with Egypt, and the prophet characterizes the politicians with a quote that he puts in their mouth, but
which they certainly did not really speak. It is a polemic
intending to characterize their real attitude. The word of doom
begins with imagery concerning a divine building Yahweh will
construct on Zion, and mentions the construction tools
"justice" and "righteousness." It is difficult to say just what this
image means; perhaps one can (and probably should) simply
circumscribe it in a general way. Yahweh will establish a new
just and righteous order on Zion and in Jerusalem (cf 1:26), and
the cornerstone is, as the foundation stone, the beginning of
this work and an allusion to the preservation of Zion expected

by Isaiah. But this new ordering process requires the removal
of the old and corrupted in hail and flood; those are
conventional images for the theophany, appearance and
activity of God. We must once again remind ourselves that the
Assyrian is still expected on the concrete level of events, though
the prophet does not at all wish to speak about this secondary
figure here. He speaks of Yahweh's coming work of salvation on
Zion, which nonetheless is a judgment for those living there
now. And in this context we find the remark, "Who believes will
not be in haste." He is not in haste or discomfited in the face of
the coming divine action bringing *salvation*, with the inevitable
reverse side: the judgment on blasphemy and the removal of
evil. Here, however, evil is "godless" politics just as always in
Isaiah, and that means false trust and lack of faith.

The final two Isaiah texts we will mention already look back
again at that refused faith that was surprisingly offered to Judah
once again as its chance before God for survival after the dark
end of 733. The first appears to have originated immediately
under the impression of the Assyrian retreat in the year 701,
when Jersualem barely survived amidst heavy casualties and by
means of high reparation payments.

> What do you mean that you have gone up,
>   all of you, to the housetops,
> you who are full of shoutings,
>   tumultuous city, exultant town?

The prophet then portrays the devastating defeat that in fact
happened to Jerusalem, because he sees that Yahweh had a day
on which *he* stepped into action, brought Jerusalem into a
critical situation, and suspended Judah's protection.

> In that day you looked to the weapons of the House of the
> Forest, and you saw the beaches of the city of David were
> many, and you collected the waters of the lower pool, and
> you counted the houses of Jerusalem, and you broke down

the houses to fortify the wall. . . . But you did not look to
him who did it, or have regard for him who planned it long
ago.

> In that day the Lord God of hosts
>   called to weeping and mourning,
>   to baldness and girding with sackcloth;
> and behold, joy and gladness,
>   slaying oxen and killing sheep,
>   eating flesh and drinking wine.
> "Let us eat and drink,
>   for tomorrow we die."

And now the prophet need only announce the death sentence
on Israel: "Surely this iniquity will not be forgiven you till you
die." (22:1-14) Israel does not see what the hour has brought; it
is celebrating intoxicating feasts while Yahweh is calling for
lament and rituals of grief. It was for faith to see what *really*
happened; but Israel did not believe. Thus unbelief brings
blindness. One paid attention to all sorts of problems in the
city's defense and to its fortifications, and worried about
keeping them intact, but did not look to the one who was doing
it: Yahweh. The prophet now shows the difference between
belief and unbelief in the contrast between seeing and not
being able to see, between looking at unimportant, external
things instead of at what is decisive. Faith was expected to see
the saving God at work even in that catastrophic occurrence—
and to depend on him. Now, after the catastrophic defeat in
which the country of Judah for all practical purposes
disappeared and only Jerusalem remained "like a lodge in the
cucumber field" (1:8)—now total blindness shows itself in the
intoxicating festivals during the period of mourning.

   We encounter a piece of this prophetic "testament" in the
final Isaiah selection concerning faith. It stands in a larger
context, however, and we will need to cite a few sentences for
the sake of better understanding. The saying begins with a
challenge to the prophet.

And now, go write it . . .
　　that it may be for the time to come
　　　　as a witness for ever.
For they are a rebellious people,
　　lying sons,
sons who will not hear
　　the instruction of the Lord.

The instruction of the Lord, this is what is cited in the following passage about faith, and because they have "despised this word" and "trusted in oppression and perverseness"—now the collapse comes, suddenly and totally, just as the prophet shows with imposing images. At the end there remains only another of the rubbish heaps of history.

For thus said the Lord God, the Holy One of Israel,
　　"In returning and rest you shall be saved;
　　in quietness and in trust shall be your strength."
And you would not, but you said,
"No! We will speed upon horses,"
　　therefore you shall speed away;
and "We will ride upon swift steeds,"
　　therefore your pursuers shall be swift.
A thousand shall flee at the threat of one,
　　at the threat of five you shall flee,
till you are left
　　like a flagstaff on the top of a mountain,
　　like a signal on a hill.

　　　　　　　　　　　　　　　　(30:8-17)

The word of doom again takes up the theme of distorted politics, and the word play—similar to the earlier one concerning the waters of the Euphrates—says in effect: "In this way you bring yourselves to ruin." Yahweh's past, rejected offer of salvation, however, corresponds exactly to the earlier word to Ahaz discussed at the beginning (see above pp 69 ff). This offer thus continued to be available, or was renewed in later years; now, in the retrospective citation, it finds its clearest articulation. The former warning, "If you will not believe, surely you shall not be established," was prefaced by the admonition for quietness and fearlessness; this is taken up again here in part, but now Yahweh's former statement has a pronounced positive meaning. "To be established" now means, "You shall be saved, your strength will be . . ." And the term "believe," although it does not occur here, is clearly alluded to in four terms, "returning to Yahweh," "rest," "quietness," and "trust."

"And you would not." The question arises once again—just as at the end of the Syro-Ephraimite War—concerning what will then be left except that rubbish heap of history. The answer is now no longer given with the reference to Zion, since it, too, is to be destroyed (32:9-14). There remains, however, the message that is written down "for the time to come"; that is to say, so it can be read then and—perhaps—awaken faith. The prophet has nothing concrete to say about this future, neither can anything be said now about hope, but rather only about the certainty that God remains, and that the word he has spoken through the prophet will once again have meaning and function. The prophetic faith is now focused on that in the face of the coming catastrophes.

If we once more look at the concept of faith in Isaiah, we see it was clearly no longer a private affair. It was wholly involved in important political decisions, or at least was supposed to be the basis for these decisions. It is easy to say retrospectively that Israel failed in this respect, but one can also easily see what it means if faith is suddenly to become the category of decision in great political questions. It is easy, of course, to point out that Isaiah's call to faith was not directed to a secular state, but rather to the people of God, or to the Davidic dynasty, which based its continuation on Yahweh's promise. In analogical fashion one can add that the statement "Not by might, nor by power, but by my Spirit" (Zech. 4:6) should at least be unconditionally valid in the church. But can we be satisfied with this simple juxtaposition of church and

secular state? In any case this is inadequate because Christians
are simultaneously members of Christian communities and
civil communities. The discomfiting question then remains
concerning the meaning of faith in public, political decisions.
Isaiah's concrete conclusion for his own time, the demand for
passivity, is certainly no recipe for all ages, but it is a strong
admonition for thorough reflection. And we can at least learn
from Isaiah that faith is no extra ingredient in all sorts of other
specialized decisions, not one detail among others, and not a
pious covering, but rather is the *foundation* of life and
decisions. We can see this once again in an example already
discussed. Perhaps one *should* have taken a look at the
miserable condition of Jerusalem's defense fortifications, one
had only first looked at Yahweh and his work (Isa. 22:1 ff). That
first sentence remains hypothetical because Israel did not do
the other, decisive thing. It helps little to ask whether it
theoretically could have been done at all in view of the confused
political problems known to *all* ages. Israel, after all, had the
prophets.

(B.) Deutereo-Isaiah

The prophet Deutereo-Isaiah appeared during another
historical hour. Now, around the middle of the sixth century
B.C., Israel's world is totally changed. Israel's end, long
predicted by the prophets, came decades ago, and it still
determines the consciousness as well as the existence of those
left behind. One does not do justice to this phenomenon by
reflecting retrospectively and concluding that there were
Israelites left, at least some Judeans remained in the country,
and others in Babylon in closed groups—the "end" could not be
all that bad. But this end was first a religious category, part of
the Yahweh faith, and could only afterward be measured by
political and sociological standards as well. Israel-Judah (the

people of God had long been represented only by Judah) did not lose just its political existence in the catastrophe of 587, the destruction of Jerusalem, it lost also its country—Yahweh's gift of salvation—and lost the Jerusalem Temple as the only legitimate cultic locale of the Yahweh faith, and with that it lost what had essentially established and supported its identity as Yahweh's people. It was threatened with losing its identity as Yahweh's people, and it had to try to win that back again—all this belongs in any talk about Israel's end. Beyond this, the economic and political conditions were extremely bad, and other communities would have lost their ethnic uniqueness under similar conditions and would have disappeared as a group. If this did not happen in Israel, if it maintained its essence and uniqueness or even won it back anew, then this no doubt has certain sociological presuppositions—above all, the tight communities of those who were led into exile in Babylon. The prophets, however, made the most important contribution here—first Ezekiel, then Deutereo-Isaiah. Both appeared among the exiles in Babylon, and from here there emerged then the decisive impulses in the subsequent period for the restitution of Judah and of the Jerusalem cultic community.

Meanwhile things had not progressed quite that far by the time of Deutereo-Isaiah. He is living in a resigned, weary community, which was probably still trying to preserve its uniqueness by placing a higher value on remnants of its religious customs; the celebration of the Sabbath and circumcision are particularly significant as signs of distinction. And yet they are tempted by the impressive religious environment, by the splendor of the Babylonian cult and its buildings and finally also by the political success of the Babylonian gods. Wasn't Yahweh defeated in 587? Such questions were eclipsed by the prophetic pronouncement two centuries before the end, but that does not prevent its being posed again. Is Yahweh only one among many gods? This is how it was seriously posed during the time of Deutereo-Isaiah.

The prophet's historical hour is characterized by the paltry spiritual and physical condition of a group of exiled who have during the past decades lost any hope of returning home and improving their lot. But that is not all, and for the prophet it is only a superficial view of things. The prophet sees the hour *much* differently. There are also external signs: the comet-like rise of the Persian king, Cyrus, who became the ruler of the Medean-Persian Empire at large in only a few short years, and was able to enlarge this empire even further. But one must understand these signs; for the prophet that political movement is only the sign and beginning of a much larger event Yahweh has set in motion. Yahweh will liberate his people by means of Cyrus and conquer the world; He will Himself lead his people home on the miraculous path through he desert, will turn all people to himself and step upon the throne of world rule in Jerusalem. Faith can expect this kind of enormous, worldwide and final salvation; and it is the prophet's task to announce this. First, however, he must lead the resigned people of Israel to faith, since it has a role in Yahweh's universal plan of salvation.

The business of faith is thus now the same as during the time of Isaiah. It should be able to see what is actually happening and recognize that Yahweh *alone* is at work. It however, is quite different as regards content. It will now be Yahweh's work of salvation; but Israel has forgotten how to believe this in view of the end it has had to experience. How can the prophet counter this?

First, there is the assurance he is to announce in the name of Yahweh; "You have not lost your identity as Yahweh's people." This identity was as a matter of fact anchored much more deeply than Israel believed. That journey out of Egypt with the bequest of the Promised Land, to which Israel once referred, has indeed been taken back by means of the Exile, and the congregation's cultic center—Zion as Yahweh's chosen city—is destroyed. But Israel's election is rooted deeper in history, since Yahweh chose the patriarchs, chose Abraham and with him Israel as Abraham's seed (Isa. 41:8 ff). This reminds one that the patriarch remains the representative of the whole community through all ages (see ch 1); thus Israel's election is no longer strengthened by Yahweh's past salvation deeds in her favor, but rather is secured in its creaturely existence as the posterity of Abraham, who was chosen (cf 51:1-2). The prophet by no means brackets out Israel's end in its religious significance; that continuity lies with Yahweh, not with Israel. Now, however, he tells Abraham's remaining descendants anew that the election "in Abraham" remained in effect beyond that end. As regards content, the faith expected from Israel is thus now designated as the faith in election. But that is only one side of the story, and the expectation of salvation awakened with such faith can and must be established in a completely different way in Deutereo-Isaiah. We will again look at a text to see how this is done.

> Why do you say, O Jacob,
>   and speak, O Israel,
> "My way is hid from the Lord,
>   and my right is disregarded by my God"?
> Have you not known? Have you not heard?
> The Lord is the everlasting God,
>   the Creator of the ends of the earth.
> He does not faint or grow weary,
>   his understanding is unsearchable.
> He gives power to the faint,
>   and to him who has no might he increases strength.
> Even youths shall faint and be weary,
>   and young men shall fall exhausted;
> but they who wait for the Lord shall renew their strength,
>   they shall mount up with wings like eagles,
> they shall run and not be weary,
>   they shall walk and not faint.
>
>   (40:27-31)[35]

This is the proclamation of faith to a resigned Israel in exile, an Israel introduced at the beginning with a fictionalized lament.

In this way the prophet takes up one of his listeners' problems: Yahweh does not concern himself with us, and our right to life (over against those who oppress us) is a matter of indifference to him. How can faith be supported in the face of this? The answer is surprising. The prophet does not at all refer to Yahweh's particular concern for Israel, but ventures much farther afield and speaks of God the Creator. Critics have wanted te explain this seemingly extraneous theological gesture by suggesting the prophet was embarrassed before his skeptical listeners when confronted with more contemporary matters—Yahweh's past salvation deeds on *Israel's* behalf—since as a matter of fact these had fallen from memory in the wake of Yahweh's judgment. But when Deutereo-Isaiah now speaks repeatedly and emphatically about Yahweh the Creator, the theological reasoning behind this concerns above all the beginning future and worldwide work of salvation. The universal dimension of Yahweh's salvation work also includes concern for the individual. The creator Yahweh has always been and is now at work, everywhere, untiringly, and with incalculable insight. Israel's lamenting question is thus answered only indirectly, or is rather transcended, since Israel's fate is, of course, also known in this God. But the prophet goes one step farther. He addresses Israel's situation when he speaks about the creator God who gives power to the faint, and when he finally calls Israel to faith with an even more powerful example. Young people can be exhausted, but those who wait for the Lord shall renew their strength; symbolically, they shall mount up with wings like eagles.

This famous and much-quoted phrase has found numerous spiritualizing interpretations; people have thought, for example, about the power of faith to raise itself above all obstacles. That is easy to misunderstand if one does not ee it in its proper context. The power of the tired and suffering is not their own free- flight, but is rather a power that comes to them: the tireless creator God *gives* power to the faint. The power of faith thus has a foundation, and with it a goal; it is not simply a waiting "for something," but rather for Yahweh. He has announced salvation through the mouth of the prophet and thus also has named the goal toward which faith that hopes in Yahweh is already moving. Israel knows this creator God from its hymns, but it must be reminded again of this foundation of its faith.

The Hebrew word for "believe" appears in another context in Deutero-Isaiah. It is in one of his judgment speeches, which portrays the scene of a trial. The case being heard is Yahweh's uniqueness as *the* God, and thus all peoples are gathered together in the scene and are supposed to present proofs for the divinity of their gods. Yahweh's proof, however, is his people Israel, and Israel is thus called up to the proceedings.

> Bring forth the people who are blind, yet have eyes,
>   who are deaf, yet have ears!
> Let all the nations gather together. . . .
> "You are my witnesses," says the Lord,
>   "and my srvant whom I have chosen,
> that you may know and believe me
>   and understand that I am He.
> Before me no god was formed,
>   nor shall there be any after me.
> I, I am the Lord,
>   and besides me there is no savior."
>   (Isa. 43:8ff)

The chosen scene does not merely serve to illustrate a theological truth, but rather also intends something very real: the moment when Yahweh's uniqueness is proven before all the world. This happens through Yahweh's saving deed on Israel's behalf, announced through the prophets, and thus is is also valid as a blind and deaf witness at the trial. That is to say, this saving deed also happens to a blind and deaf Israel, and happens "that *you* may believe." We now encounter a stylistic break in

the trial speech; one would expect all the people to believe at
this point. But this break is intentional. First, Israel is to accept
what Yahweh does on its behalf, and—unlike the announcement of doom before—it matters that Israel agrees and
believes. It will, however, be a retroactive faith here in view of
the saving event, and faith will then lie on the same level with
knowing and understanding. The content of this faith is that
there is only one God (the oriental divine genealogies thus
being excluded). This does not, however, remain simply an
abstract doctrine, but rather is immediately concretized. Only
one saves; that is what matters (cf also Isa. 45:21 et passim.).

Yahweh's saving work is in the final analysis directed
toward the whole world, but it happens first on behalf of Israel.
Yahweh's reasoning is as exclusive as his acts; it resides only
with God, not with Israel. The prophet makes this clear in a trial
speech in which Yahweh defends himself against Israel's
complaints and simultaneously raises a counter complaint. He
rejects Israel's suggestion that it has a right to Yahweh's saving
action because of its heavy sacrifices before the Exile:

> I have not burdened you with offerings,
>   or wearied you with frankincense. . . .
> But you have burdened me with your sins,
>   you have wearied me with your iniquities.
>
> I, I am He
>   who blots out your transgressions for my own sake,
>   and I will not remember your sins.
>   (Isa. 43:23*b*-25)

As regards both Israel's sins and its sacrifices, this is a speech
about past things; yet these things must be discussed now
because one cannot simply disregard sin, since sin produces
effects and misfortune extending on into the present. Yahweh
does not "forget" them, but rather blots them out. That is to say,

he eliminates them and their consequences. That is the toil
Israel has given him. A similar phrase makes it clear why
Yahweh does this.

> For my own sake, for my own sake, I do it,
>   for how should my name be profaned?
> My glory I will not give to another.
>   (Isa. 48:11)

This kind of explanation for Yahweh's salvation acts has a
tradition behind it, and we encounter it already in Ezekiel
(particularly 36:22; cf 20:9, 14, 22, 44), and it contains a deep
theological meaning. If salvation is to be certain, then it must be
grounded in God and not in men. If Yahweh is acting for the
sake of his name and glory, he does so because he has bound
himself to this people and acts in their behalf with his own glory
at stake. The *same* idea can, however, be articulated in a
different way—much more strongly focused on man—when
Yahweh gives the reason for his salvation act: "Because you are
precious in my eyes, and honored, and I love you" (Isa. 43:4).
This is naturally not speaking about some quality unique to
Israel, but rather about an appreciation and love coming to it
from Yahweh. How can it be otherwise, since the prophet must
after all speak with great seriousness about the deeply rooted
sinfulness? Even "your first father sinned" (43:27), that is: You
are a sinner from the very foundation of your existence (cf again
Ezek. 20, but also already Hos. 11; 12:3 ff).

Using Israel's relationship with God as a model, all this
leads to an understanding of the relationship between God and
man that was later taken up in the Pauline-reformed view of
justification *sola gratia* ("by grace alone"), and had to be further
thought out within the understanding of God's new act of
salvation. One can then see there is not (yet) any talk here about
justification by faith (Rom. 3:28), indeed "faith" is not even
mentioned in these texts. But it was expected, and it was the

prophet's task to assemble an unbelieving Israel around the God who was bringing forth salvation, "to bring Jacob back to him" (49:5). Faith, however, was to come about in this kind of turning to Yahweh (cf Isa. 30:15). Faith was for Deutereo-Isaiah (as for Paul) not the basis and presupposition of the divine salvation work, but was rather to come essentially "afterward", as man's answer and reaction to the experienced salvation. No doubt he also had to speak to his listeners about a future that was certain although not yet visible on earth, and he had to expect faith that trusted in the word of God. However, unlike Isaiah, in Deutero-Isaiah we find no more mention of a judgment upon unbelief.

We also find no more mention of this "afterward" quality of faith in the text ending our journey through the Old Testament. It was probably composed later by Deutero-Isaiah's followers and contains a bit of the prophet's own style, but it goes beyond that and speaks extensively about God's work. We once again encounter the term *hä'ämin* ("believe"), but this time used in an extremely peculiar fashion. It occurs in a piece from the last servant song (Isa. 52:13–53:12). In the middle piece (53:1-10/11a), however, a chorus still to come is speaking:

Who has believed what we have heard?
    And to whom has the arm of the Lord been revealed?
For he grew up before him like a young plant,
    and like a root out of dry ground;
he had no form or comeliness that we should look at him,
    and no beauty that we should desire him.
He was despised and rejected by men;
    a man of sorrows, and acquainted with grief. . . .

Surely he has borne our griefs
    and carried our sorrows;
yet we esteemed him stricken,
    smitten by God, and afflicted. . . .
All we like sheep have gone astray;
    we have turned every one to his own way;

and the Lord has laid on him
   the iniquity of us all.

                                          (53:1-6)

And then, after the portrayal of his shameful fate until death, we
read:

Yet it was the will of the Lord to bruise him;
   he has put him to grief;
when he makes himself an offering for sin,
   he shall see his offspring, he shall prolong his days;
the will of the Lord shall prosper in his hand.

                                          (53:10)

This great passage cannot be exegeted here, so we will only
mention a few fundamental characteristics. There is talk of
God's salvation work that comes about in an unbelievable way.
The account of the lowliness and elevation of the servant is
already looking back from the time of the servant's elevation,
though for the text's author it is still future; he begins with
Yahweh's word about the future in Isaiah 52:13-15 (the
beginning of this text) and tells about the moment in which all
the world will be astonished and see what has happened. Then
they will say, "Who believed?" and that is not much different
than saying "Who would have thought that possible?" No one
would have thought it possible, but now the "arm of the Lord,"
the proof of power in this servant, has been revealed in the
miserable figure who suffered for others so that salvation might
come to "the many." God was with that suffering one. The
supplicants in the Psalms had already experienced that, those
who fled from the distant, hidden God to the near, revealed
one. But now we read: God recognizes the suffering of his
servant who guided God's work to its goal, not only by means of
his proclamation, but also by means of his own fate. That is—it
says—unbelievable; one can, however, see it in retrospect. We
thus conclude the Old Testament account of faith with this
element of "unbelief."

Retrospect

A real summary is not in order here; it would only shorten and abridge what according to the Old Testament can only be portrayed in texts. Anyone who has made the journey along this long path into such different areas of the Old Testament can, however, recall some of the important experiences. We consciously did not proceed according to a particular concept, but rather took the most convenient Old Testament word for "believe" as a guide. It acquires that particular pregnant meaning only in certain contexts, above all in Isaiah and in Genesis 15:6. A multiplicity of other verbs, however, aid in characterizing the phenomenon: to hope and wait, to shelter oneself and seek refuge, and above all to trust. Faith always includes trust, and there is no faith in the Old Testament without trust. It is, however, more than just that, or is something more precise. It is the kind of trust in God which can—in principal—be expressed and articulated. This does not exclude the possibility that even the believer may often be silent in the midst of great suffering, but he completes the turn to faith by turning to the familiar God. He is able to call on experiences with this God that he or others before him have had; only for this reason is lament possible and meaningful. Faith in a situation of need has its basis in past saving experiences, and it reaches out anew for that deliverance which is expected even when appearances indicate disaster. This certainty of faith comes to expression in statements of trust and in reference to past and future praise of God. Here, in the Psalms, one thus finds a text book of the language of faith.

Israel formed models of faith in its narratives about its ancestor Abraham. From the earliest times Israel worked on this model and brought in the nomadic experiences of its ancestors. Here, too, faith is always trust in the familiar God, but is it also articulated trust? Abraham nowhere speaks a confession of faith; whenever he speaks he more often expresses skepticism, and his faith appears as a silent obedience. But his faith "articulates" itself acoustically; he listens for the God who manifests himself in the promise. He must even hold this promise to be true when what seems to be its only realization is again to be taken back. He believed in the God for whom "nothing is too miraculous," the God who performs miracles.

This is also the basis of faith in Isaiah. Faith sees what is *really* happening in history and what is *really* important. When faith here first becomes a matter of public importance and is to guide political decisions, the difference from the Abraham stories is above determined by the different form of society. There the whole community was represented by the small group, by the clan with its ancestor who determined "politics"; now the larger civil community has replaced it, a community which in the middle of other oriental states was forced to make its decisions much more strongly according to pragmatic considerations. Judah was not a secular state, but it did in fact pursue secular politics (which, as is well-known, does not exclude emotions). With the renewal of the announcement of salvation, Israel stood before the decison between belief and unbelief. Belief would now need to prove itself by means of reserve, by letting God act; this is what is meant by "passivity." That is the most difficult thing to do. What faith is then expected to *do* is the lesser problem. The Israel of Isaiah's time did not believe, and in view of the grievous catastrophes the prophet sees coming, faith must now be understood radically. It sees God perform the strange deed (Isa. 28:21), and it must leave the future completely in the hands of its God. In the catastrophic events it also sees its God at work as the judging and saving God.

The second prophet, Deutero-Isaiah, summarized this in a pregnant sentence when he concluded Yahweh's oracle to Cyrus in the following way:

I form light and create darkness,
I make weal and create woe,
I am the Lord, who do all these things.
(Isa. 45:7)

Israel only has one God, not two, to whom it can attribute the devastation. Israel's faith was expected to endure that, and was thus confronted with its most difficult task. For Deutero-Isaiah such problems are solved by the certainty that God is now creating salvation, that he is now performing his great work of salvation that no unbelief will be able to stop and that faith can only follow. This God acts "for his own sake." Salvation is grounded in him and he finally guides it to its goal by means of the suffering and failing of his servant.

B.
FAITH
IN THE
NEW TESTAMENT

I. Earliest Christianity: Faith in the Crucified and Risen Christ

1. The Oldest Christian Confession

Earliest Christianity picks up the word "faith," which had come down to it through the Old Testament and the traditions of Judaism, and uses it to characterize that conviction which held and supported it. For Christianity just as for ancient Israel, faith means confident trust that depends on God's promise, a promise given through his word, which is itself spoken reliably to his community. This word is not, however, spoken in this or that sentence, but is rather authenticated for all time in the gospel. The news of God's love is carried forth by proclaiming as good news the event through which God manifested his mercy in Christ. Faith says yes to this message and accepts it by recognizing it as true. It thereby comprehends that this proclamation concerns it in an unconditional manner because this proclamation offers an answer to the never-silent question concerning the meaning and goal of our life.

The oldest literary document preserved from early Christianity is the first letter to the congregation in Thessalonica, composed in the year A.D. 50. The apostle Paul is writing to the young congregation, which only a short time before had come into being as a result of his activity, and he speaks here about the faith binding Christians together. He offers as the content of this faith the fact "that Jesus died and rose again" (1 Thess. 4:14). He summarizes in these few words what it is that establishes and fulfills faith. He refers to a particular event designated by the name Jesus of Nazareth, his death, and his resurrection. Every person can learn about the event which was his death; this, however, does not yet give rise to faith, but rather only offers a particular knowledge. Faith announces that in this event God has acted, and that it knows itself to be involved. God did not leave Jesus in death, but rather resurrected him. The truth of this statement can be established neither through investigation nor through attentive interest. It is comprehended rather only in a faith that puts its trust in the fact that God himself is speaking to us through the crucified and resurrected Jesus of Nazareth. From this brief reference to the content and basis of faith the apostle Paul therefore immediately draws the conclusion in that letter he writes to Thessalonica. If we believe that Jesus died and rose again, then we are ourselves drawn into this event; that is to say: "Even so, through Jesus, God will bring with him those who have fallen asleep." By this Paul means that all who have put their trust in Christ as their Lord and have died with this conviction, will rise from death into life with Jesus. They are to be joined with him in that triumphal procession that will unite all who belong to the Lord (1 Thess. 4:13-18). Thus the oldest written account which speaks about Christian faith is not concerned with faith in and for itself, but rather interprets faith in a way encompassing Christ and those who belong to Christ, and so spans past, present, and future. Whoever believes in Christ gains confidence for his path through life. He recognizes which task is put to him in the world, and goes about the business of fulfilling this task as well as he is able.

That short sentence, "We believe that Jesus died and rose again," needs further commentary because in this compressed form it represents an abridged version, no doubt comprehensible to Christians among themselves, but which they have to explain to others. In the earliest Christian proclamation this exegesis was taken up and placed into the congregation's confession. The apostle Paul presents a pedagogical summary of this proclamation at the beginning of the fifteenth chapter of his first letter to the congregation in Corinth. This writing originated around the middle of the 50s, only a short time after the First Letter to the Thessalonians. Paul is reminding the community in these sentences about the message he once brought to them when he first came to the city and delivered the words about Christ. The apostle does not quote its content with his own words, but rather in a formulation which he—as he assures them—has himself already accepted. Thus this tradition must reach back into the first beginnings of Christianity. It goes as follows: "that Christ died for our sins in accordance with the scriptures, that he was buried, that he was raised on the third day in accordance with the scriptures, and that he appeared to Cephas, then to the twelve" (1 Cor. 15:3-5).[36] The Corinthians accepted this message and are supposed to remain with it—"unless you believed in vain" (v 2). Thus here, too, it is a matter of drawing the necessary conclusions from the faith for which one has made a decision. The apostle then describes these conclusions in detail in the extensive discussion about the proper understanding of the resurrection of the dead. But before he gets into this discussion, he emphasizes the conviction common to all Christians.

The death and resurrection of Jesus Christ are designated in this tradition—just as in the brief citation in the First Letter to the Thessalonians—as the central content of the Christian confession. Their meaning is explained in a few words in the tradition Paul cites, a meaning which deserves closer consideration.[37] One should first notice that right at the beginning it is not the name "Jesus of Nazareth" that is given, but rather the title "Christ." According to its original meaning it refers to the anointed one who has been chosen by God for a royal office and placed into power. At the end-time this anointed one of God is to appear according to the model of King David, liberate his enslaved people and lead them into the time of salvation. But nowhere in the eschatological expectation of Judaism is there talk about the Messiah suffering, dying, and taking the people's sins upon himself. For this reason, this first statement of the Christian confession already had to arouse alienation and consternation in Jewish listeners: the Christ was crucified and died. He suffered death to the bitter end, and was buried just as every dead person is laid into the earth.

How could it happen that the Messiah did not appear in splendor and glory, but rather gave his life on the cross? For an explanation of this the Christian proclamation referred from the very beginning to the writings of the Old Testament, and this reference is put into effect for the cross as well as for the resurrection of Christ. This does not just mean this or that individual Old Testament passage is cited, but rather that the entire scripture is claimed as an explanation of the gospel. To be sure, in the passion story and in connection with the passages about Jesus' death on the cross, individual sections of the Old Testament are presented more frequently: Psalms 22, 31, and 69, and above all the song of the suffering servant from Isaiah 53. These passages represent, however, all of scripture, whose hidden meaning reveals itself only from the perspective of the message of Christ. Similarly, one does not think of this or that individual Old Testament statement in the remark that Christ's resurrection occurred on the third day according to scrip- ture—that is, after a short period of time—one offers rather all of scripture from the beginning to end as a witness for Christ's resurrection.

Christ died for our sins. This sentence states what faith confesses concerning Christ's cross. Aside from the reference to scripture, no explanation is given here of why Christ's death represents atonement for sins. The decisive statement, however, is clearly formulated: our own sins, our remoteness from God caused by our guilt, are the reason Christ had to suffer and die. He stepped into the gap we are unable to close ourselves. He did this, however, in order to take away our sins that we might become free. Paul later expresses this thought in the following way, "For our sake he made him to be sin who knew no sin, so that in him we might become the righteousness of God" (2 Cor. 5:21).

Christ suffered and died that we might receive forgiveness of sins. His death was no accidental or tragic event, but rather God's will. Christ's cross is visible to every person and can be ascertained as an historical occurrence at the time of the Roman administrator Pontius Pilate in Palestine.[38] But no investigation can prove that God's mercy was revealed there; only in faith can it be recognized, in faith that recognizes Christ in the crucified one and confesses him as the living Lord. Thus the meaning of the sentence that speaks of the significance of Jesus's death can only be comprehended in connection with the statement about the risen Christ, since only in the closest mutual relationship can Jesus' death and his resurrection be properly understood. Christ's death has the inherent power to establish and give salvation because he was awakened from death. "If Christ has not been raised," Paul says to the Corinthians, "then our preaching is in vain and your faith is in vain" (1 Cor. 15:17).

Without Easter, Good Friday would only signify the end of Jesus' path, not deliverance and life. Jesus of Nazareth, however, is not proclaimed as the Christ in *spite* of the death he had to suffer, but rather precisely because of his death he is confessed as the Messiah who is resurrected on the third day. The earliest Christian proclamation gives no information about the details of this occurrence, but merely mentions the unprecedented event as such. Christ rose again according to scripture, and appeared to Cephas and the Twelve. It is not said where and how this occurred. What is decisive is that they were taken into his service as witnesses. Their preaching stands at the beginning of the church: that God spoke the last word and granted victory to life at the very place where death and the grave appeared to have established an irrevocable end. Whoever hears this word from the gospel and accepts it, that person believes and is thus a Christian.

2. Faith in Christ

The gospel, proclaimed as the good news and accepted in faith, is proclaimed in agreement by the earliest community and by Paul. "So we preached and so you believed," he thus calls out to the Corinthians (1 Cor. 15:11). This agreement must by no means, however, be formulated continually in the same terminology, but is rather grounded in the universally Christian understanding of the one gospel whose content can very well be expressed in various ways. At the beginning of the Letter to the Romans, in which he introduces himself to the congregation, known to him personally, in the empire's capital, Paul thus refers to the gospel upon which faith in Christ bases itself. The early Christian statement cited by him deals with Christ, the Son of God and our Lord: "who was descended from David according to the flesh and designated Son of God in power according to the Spirit of holiness by his resurrection from the dead" (Rom. 1:3 ff).[39] In this citation it is not death and resurrection, but rather Christ's earthly existence and heavenly splendor that stand juxtaposed. His earthly activity is characterized by his Davidic sonship, but he is designated the Son of God as the one resurrected. According to the early Christian understanding, this fulfilled what was announced in Psalm 2:7. God spoke to the anointed one, "You are my son, today I have begotten you." These words bestow the ruling office upon the chosen one. The believers confess their belief in him, the Son of David and Son of God, as their Lord, and thus say, "Jesus Christ our Lord" (Rom. 1:4).

In this sentence faith brings to expression who Jesus of Nazareth is. In this judgment it differentiates itself from other opinions expressed about him. Some—so say the writers of the Gospels—see in him John the Baptist whom Herod had executed (Mark 6:14-29, par). Others consider him to be the prophet Elijah, who is to come again at the end of days as the

messenger of God. And some think he is one of the prophets
who proclaim what the God of Israel says (Mark 8:27 ff, par). A
great respect and appreciation is expressed in these statements.
The highest titles of honor are attributed to Jesus, titles with
which one designated men sent by God. The decisive question,
however, one put to Jesus' disciples, is the following, "But who
do you say that I am?" As the spokesman for the disciples, Peter
answers with the confession: "You are the Christ" (Mark 8:29,
par). The gospel writer immediately adds the christological
teaching "that the Son of man must suffer many things, and be
rejected by the elders and the chief priests and the scribes, and
be killed, and after three days rise again" (Mark 8:31, par). This
contradicts other views according to which the Messiah title
might refer to the victorious ruler of the people, and
unambiguously present and argues for the Christian understanding of Christ's title of honor. The Christ was nailed to the
cross, died, was buried, raised on the third day, and showed
himself as the Living One to his followers.

Whoever believes in the risen Christ receives salvation—
this is how it is expressed in the early Christian confession cited
by Paul in the Letter to the Romans: "Because if you confess
with your lips that Jesus is Lord and believe in your heart that
God raised him from the dead, you will be saved" (Rom. 10:9).
On the one hand, in this tightly parallel statement the two
conditional clauses correspond: "if you confess"—"if you
believe." Confession and faith are tightly bound together, since
faith is stated in a binding way in the public expression of the
confession. On the other hand, however, the two references to
content belong intimately together: "Jesus is Lord"—"God
raised him from the dead." Whoever believes in the crucified
and risen Christ confesses him as Lord. And reversed: Only he
who has accepted the preaching of the resurrection from the
dead can confess Christ as Lord. This confession is expressed in
the worship service assembly with the cry: "Jesus is Lord" (1
Cor. 12:3), or "Jesus Christ is Lord" (Phil. 2:11). Only he is able

to agree with this cry who has been seized by the power of the Spirit and through it recognizes the criucified Christ as Lord (1 Cor. 12:1-3).

Faith thus does not emerge on the basis of critical reflection and judgment, but rather from the preaching that proclaims Christ and thus awakens faith (Rom. 10:17). So one does not come to faith by considering from a critical distance the news of the occurrence of Jesus' death on the cross and the resurrection, and then deciding what position one wishes to take concerning it. The preaching naturally contains information about the history of Jesus, but it takes it up into the exhortation that this event happened for us. It is seen as the act of God, because he raised Jesus from the dead and made him Lord of all Lords. A faith that accepts this message and takes it as the appropriation of salvation is thus always faith in the God who let himself be recognized for what he is through the resurrection of Christ from the dead. The content of faith, and faith as process, are inseparably connected, since the proclamation's truth is recognized only in the trusting agreement with the message of the gospel.[40] Ground would be lost if one wanted to separate this trust, based on the message spoken to him, from this context.

"Believing in Christ Jesus" (Gal. 2:16) thus means the same as "believing that Jesus died and rose" (1 Thess. 4:14 and elsewhere). The content of faith can be given, on the one hand, by a "that"clause pointing to the event of the cross and resurrection of Christ, and on the other hand, by the short phrase "in Christ." The two manners of expression do not differ in their objective content, but rather agree in meaning.[41] The Christian faith, just as the faith of Israel in the Old Testament, is related to an act of God to whose present validity the people in turn confess; but it goes beyond the understanding of faith available in the writings of the Old Testament in that it relates to the Christ-event as God's revelation of mercy, which has now occurred once and for all. Whoever confesses that he believes in Christ thus says that God himself encounters us in Christ, and indeed even more: that only in the crucified and risen Christ does God reveal who he is.[42]

Faith in Christ should not be misunderstood as if it were a particular idea which, with the aid of faith, might be made legitimate, but otherwise would be considered only barely possible. Faith does not just enter the picture when, for example, the examining and evaluating capacity of reason reaches its limits or finds it must consider certain information doubtful and unbelievable. Faith rather knows itself to be seized by Christ. It would thus be contrary to the meaning of Christian faith if one wanted to employ it only when there is a lack of proof for this or that statement.[43] Faith in Christ is totally different from this kind of alleged faith, since in the face of the crucified and risen Lord it unconditionally trusts God's word of love spoken to it, and thus puts its trust not in this or that objective content, but alone in Christ the Lord.

3. The Community of Believers

Only the individual person can give the answer of faith by which the gospel is accepted. However, by means of this answer he also becomes a member of the community which assembles as the people of God, and he belongs to the convocation of believers. In the New Testament the Christians are frequently referred to simply as the believers.[44] Whenever one speaks about the Christians in Achaia and Macedonia, one speaks about the believers (1 Thess. 1:7), and in Corinth one differentiates between believers and non-believers (1 Cor. 6:6; 14:22 ff; and elsewhere). In Acts the believers—or those who have come to faith—are often mentioned in order to characterize the Christian community (Acts 2:44; 4:32; 15:5; 18:27; 19:18; 21:20). The name "Christians" did not originate in Jerusalem, but rather in Antioch, and was first given to the members of the community by those outside it (Acts 11:26). The fact that they confess Christ as Lord leads this faith to be judged as something which characterizes the entire conduct and demeanor of their lives.

The Christians read the Old Testament as their Holy Scripture just as did the Jews, and the first Christian communities continually emphasized that the death and resurrection of Jesus Christ—which the gospel proclaims as proof of God's love—happened according to scripture and were thus the fulfillment of the Old Testament promises. They consciously wanted to maintain Israel's inheritance and thus called up scripture as witness.

This understanding continues a strand that was already distinctly developed in the Judaism of the period, since in the middle of an environment which believed differently than they, the Jews had to come to a sense of certainty about what the foundation of their life and actions was. The concept of faith plays an important role in this entire discussion which Judaism had to confront during the hellenistic period.[45] Thus Josephus, a Jewish historian who lived during the first century after Christ, speaks about faith repeatedly and with strong emphasis. He speaks there about Moses as the one who not only planted the faith in God in his contemporaries, but also in all subsequent generations.[46] By this he means the dogmatic version of Jewish faith in God that guides correct behavior and action. Talk about faith also finds special emphasis in the thought of the Jewish philosopher Philo of Alexandria, who likewise lived during the first century of the Christian Era and sought a synthesis between Old Testament tradition and Greek thought.[47] He juxtaposes faith with a trust that relates to secular things, and because that faith is directed only to God, it is even to be considered the peer of wisdon. Just as wisdom turns away from all earthly things and directs itself toward the heavenly world, so also does faith bid farewell to false opinions and trusts God as the only one who remains steadfast and unchangeable.[48]

When Philo describes wisdom's behavior as faith and calls it the highest of all virtues, he is interpreting the biblical concept before him in a way rendering it comprehensible for Greek thought. This agreement, however, was not primarily intended to serve the development of missionary activity in the hellenistic world, but was rather supposed to help the Jewish community reflect upon the behavior that was pleasing to God and thus be able to live that faith in the middle of a world that had different beliefs than they.[49] For this reason the concept of faith is not employed in conversion sermons directed toward outsiders, but has its place rather within the framework of deliberations held within the Jewish community for the purpose of describing the essence and content of Judaism.

In other Jewish documents during the New Testament period, talk about faith is supposed to give information about the foundations of a pious life. Thus the Greek version of the book of Jesus Sirach speaks about a trusting faith in the Lord or in the law (35 [32]:24; 36 [33]:3). In these concept clusters, one can see that according to Jewish understanding the relationship to God is determined by one's relationship to the law. Faith in God can only arise within obedience to the law. The Fourth Book of Maccabees—which emerged sometime around the time of Christ's birth in the Jewish Diaspora, perhaps in Alexandria or Syria-Asia Minor—also speaks about faith as the conduct of those who know themselves to be bound to the law (4:7; 7:19, 21; 8:7; 15:24; 16:22; 17:2; and elsewhere).[50] And the Syrian Apocalypse of Baruch mentions those "who are without blemish, who have subjected themselves in faith to you and your Law" (54:5). "To have works and faith in the All-highest and Almighty" (4 Ezra 13:23) is the condition for being saved from the final afflictions. Trusting in God—according to the doctrine of the Jewish community in Qumran on the shores of the Dead Sea—can only be maintained by turning to the Law of Moses and obediently following the interpretation given it by the Teacher of Righteousness.[51] This brings faith into a secure relationship with the law, which as God's guidance determines the life of the believers. Through the law, God has announced to his people what he has to say, and Israel thus witnesses to its faith by acting according to the law and fulfilling its commandments.[52]

The Greek and Roman world, on the other hand, was not familiar with the idea of faith in a deity. The gods spoken of in that religious tradition are understood as lords of that order obtaining in nature who insure that the destiny of the state makes the proper course. The respect due them is shown by paying cultic homage and punctually bringing the required sacrifices. But there is no talk of a faith which directs its trust to the one God or to the majority of divine powers.[53] When oriental religions became known in Greece and Rome during the waning years of antiquity, many people were initiated into the cults of Serapis, Isis, Osiris, and other gods, cults which did not mutually exclude one another. It was on the contrary quite acceptable to join several such Mystery communities in order to heighten the consecrated power they promised to deliver. There was no cultivation of a confession that would have meant a strict binding in faith to a single diety. Membership in a religious community was based rather on cultic initiation and consummated by participation in worship service assemblies to which only initiated mystogogues were admitted.[54]

As a means of developing its own understanding of faith, earliest Christianity did not turn to hellenistic concepts and ideas, but rather employed and carried forth the language it found before it in the Old Testament and in Judaism. Just as the Jewish communities, in the middle of a world that believed differently than they, had to come to some clarity about what they had to hold onto, so also did the first Christians have to answer the question concerning the basis of their confidence. In this process Christ, not the law, was designated as the object and content of faith; the community's trust directed itself to him. Since the Christians laid claim to the Scriptures for their gospel, they had to come into a dispute with the Jews on this topic.[55] Although there were occasionally sharp debates between Jews and Christians concerning the proper understanding of scripture, those initial Christian communities always held firm the notion that there are not different manners of faith, but rather only the one faith witnessed by scripture as promise and brought to fulfillment by the gospel. This is why they never ceased soliciting Israel's acceptance of the message of Christ; the community of believers was never permitted to cut off the dialogue concerning faith they were to carry on with the Israel of the old covenant, since they—like the Jews—also confessed the God of Abraham, Isaac, and Jacob who makes the dead living.

II. The Synoptic Gospels: Faith as Trust in God

1. Faith in the Encounter with Jesus

The Gospels often mention the fact that faith is awakened in the encounter with Jesus.[56] Faith is called the hoping expectation with which a person in need turns to Jesus and asks for help. We thus hear of those who lay a lame person at his feet so that he may turn away the affliction (Mark 2:5), and we are told how sick and suffering people come to Jesus in their helplessness. Jesus addresses them and tells them that their faith—even if it is weak and hesitating—will save them (Mark 5:36; par and elsewhere). Others ask Jesus for help for their servant or child (Matt. 8:13; par and Luke 7:10; Mark 9:23 ff, par). Their requests are granted because they trust in the fact that Jesus can help.

These stories, however, do not represent reports that tell directly what happened during the ministry of Jesus of Nazareth, but rather, they were written down decades later. Jesus himself did not write down a single word, and there is no direct tradition preserved about him. Before the Gospels were composed one told orally what was known of Jesus and who this Lord is who is proclaimed by the gospel as the crucified and risen Christ. Every bit of information giving accounts about him was transmitted orally by Christians who confessed him. The gospel writers, who pick up and articulate this orally transmitted tradition, are not primarily concerned with preserving past events. To be sure, they show a clear interest in the history of Jesus, but above all they want to show that Jesus is the present Lord. His community trusts in his word and lives according to his guidance. Thus the account of what once happened is encompassed and stamped by the Christian confession, since the gospel writers want to portray how Jesus preached and ministered, and thus show how his proclamation was taken up by the community.

The evangelist Mark, who was the first to produce a written portrayal of Jesus' ministry shortly before A.D. 70, emphasizes his book's topic already in the first sentence, "The gospel of Jesus Christ" (Mark 1:1). He thereby takes up the old Christian concept of gospel (1 Cor. 15:3-5; Rom. 1:3 ff), and thus wants to be a co-worker in the universally Christian task of preaching the good news. It corresponds to this understanding that the passion narrative, even as regards external dimensions, emerges as the most important part of Jesus' ministry. The evangelist extends the concept of the gospel backward—a concept originally related only to the proclamation of the cross and resurrection of Christ—in that he sees the beginning of the gospel of Jesus Christ to be given with the appearance of John the Baptist and the beginning of Jesus' own ministry. Whatever is told of Jesus is interpreted from the perspective of the central content of the Christian proclamation. Thus the stories which tell of encounters with Jesus are to illustrate how the gospel reaches men in their day-to-day lives and brings them onto the path of being followers of Jesus. Thus the Gospels are fundamentally not to be read any differently than the early Christian letters and other New Testament writings: as presentations of the one message about Christ that is proclaimed to Jews and Greeks as an offer of God's mercy. Their unique character resides in the fact that they develop this message with a backward look to the history of Jesus.

With what right, however, do the evangelists not only present their message as the preaching of the cross and resurrection of Jesus Christ, but also pull the history of Jesus of Nazareth into the proclamation?[57] Just as did the authors of the other early Christian writings, so also do the gospel writers want to show that only he who encounters the resurrected Lord and is addressed by his word[58] is able to comprehend the correct meaning of what Jesus said and did. But the resurrected Christ is identical with the Jesus of Nazareth who once ministered in Galilee and Jerusalem. Christian faith is not referring to some mythical being, but rather to Jesus of Nazareth. Thus the question must be posed concerning who this Jesus was, and what he preached and did. First of all the gospel writers' histories give information about what the believing community transmitted about its Lord, and how they saw and understood Jesus several decades after his ministry. Some sentences and sections in the Gospels cannot be traced back to Jesus himself, but are rather influenced by the languages of the confessing community. Thus the Christians were unable to speak about Jesus' suffering, death, and resurrection except from the perspective of the events of Good Friday and Easter. For this reason all sentences which deal with his passion and resurrection have been formed by the Christian confession (Mark 8:31; par; 9:31; par; 10:33 ff; par;

and elsewhere). Citations and allusions to Old Testament scripture, which frequently arise within the passion narrative, correspond to the conviction that Jesus' death and resurrection happened "according to scripture" (1 Cor. 15:3-5). Since the Christian community needed directions for correct behavior, Jesus' words were collected together as larger compositions which thus took on the characteristics of catechisms. We find such compositions, for example, in the field sermon (Luke 6:20-49) or in the much more extensive Sermon on the Mount (Matt. 5–7). They do not recount speeches of Jesus that were actually given, but rather emerged only later in the community tradition. The stories dealing with encounters with Jesus and with the emergence of faith also received their contours from the proclamation and doctrine of the community.

But how did encounters with Jesus occur at that time when he was preaching in Galilee and Jerusalem? And what did Jesus himself say? If that level of tradition which can be considered the oldest one, ultimately going back to Jesus, is to be separated from the portrayals given by the Christian community and the gospel writer, then we need unambiguous criteria that will aid in clarifying which words without doubt go back to Jesus, and not to the transmitting community or the formulation of one of the gospel writers. Those sayings can be considered to be such sentences which, on the one hand, can be differentiated from the statements of confessing faith as formed by the community, and which, on the other hand, are thrown into distinct relief against the background of contemporary Jewish ideas. There can, of course, be no doubt that Jesus of Nazareth also used Jewish phrases or spoke sentences that touch on or are exactly the same as the community's confessional formulations. An analysis of the tradition preserved in the Gospels, however, must first be carried through with the aid of these critical standards in order to gain as firm a basis as possible. Then, with the aid of the results gained in this way, the rest of the tradition can be investigated and related to that original point of departure.[59] The Christian faith confessing Jesus of Nazareth as the Christ of God is interested in clarifying the question concerning what Jesus himself said about faith. Only then can one see clearly what relationship the Christian confession has to the call that went out from Jesus.[60]

In some passages one can easily see that certain statements about faith are formulations of the community or of the gospel writers. This is how the evangelist Mark takes up the thematic designation, placed at the beginning of his book, again into the summarizing characterization of Jesus' preaching (1:15). Jesus announces the near arrival of God's reign and calls out for the people to turn away from the false path and toward that divine reign. To this statement, which accurately renders what Jesus himself preached (cf Matt. 4:17; Luke 13:1-5; 15:7, 10 and elsewhere) the challenge is added: "And believe in the gospel." This manner of expression corresponds exactly to the early Christian understanding of a gospel which is asking for the assent of faith. In this form it cannot be traced back to Jesus, but rather represents a formulation of the evangelist who is speaking in the language of the believing community.

According to Mark 9:42 Jesus warned against despising or aggravating one of the little ones who believe. The evangelist Matthew expands this turn of phrase in a commentary by now advising, not to aggravate one of the little ones "who believe in me" (Matt. 18:6). In the interpretation of the parable about the four-part field, the various events described previously are explained one after the other. Seed fell on the path, but the birds came and devoured it (Mark 4:4, par). That means, the word is spread, and people listen to it. But then Satan comes and takes away the word that was sown (Mark 4:15). The evangelist Luke joins in this interpretation as it lay before him in the Gospel of Mark, but on his own part adds, "That they may not believe and be saved" (Luke 8:12). By doing this he underscores the warning given to take the message seriously and to cling to it so that salvation is not thrown away, since whenever faith departs, so also is that salvation lost to which the gospel liberates us. The evangelist thus picks up a phrase of early Christian proclamation challenging one not to despise God's word, but rather to hear it gladly and learn. This is why the warning for correct hearing is spoken. "For John came to you in the way of righteousness, and you did not believe him, but the tax collectors and the harlots believed him; and even when you saw it, you did not afterward repent and believe him" (Matt. 21:32).[61] Many of the people one would actually expect to agree with Jesus' word and follow him, instead close themselves off to this preaching that calls one to turn around. Some people, however, who are despised by the others, open themselves up to this call which they find concerns and involves them, and they believe. He who has ears to hear, let him hear! (Mark 4:9, par).

In these sentences we hear the Christian sermon that seeks to call its listeners to faith. But how did encounters with Jesus of Nazareth occur before Good Friday and Easter? And what did Jesus himself say about faith at that time? Information about this question is given by a passage that speaks of the power of faith, and it is found in various places in the Gospels.

2. The Power of Faith

A saying of Jesus' describing the incomparable power of faith is transmitted in the Synoptic Gospels in various versions. On the one hand we read, "Truly, I say to you, whoever says to this mountain, 'Be taken up and cast into the sea,' and does not doubt in his heart, but believes that what he says will come to pass, it will be done for him" (Mark 11:23). In the Gospel of Mark this statement by Jesus is added to the conversation he has with his disciples after the cursing of the fig tree. The evangelists Matthew and Luke, on the otherhand, took up a version from the tradition of sayings and put it into different contexts. According to the Gospel of Luke, Jesus said: "If you had faith as a grain of mustard seed, you could say to this sycamine tree, 'Be rooted up, and be planted in the sea,' and it would obey you" (Luke 17:6). And in the Gospel of Matthew Jesus' words are: "If you have faith as a grain of mustard seed, you will say to this mountain, 'Move hence to yonder place,' and it will move; and nothing will be impossible to you" (Matt. 17:20).

The scope of the tradition shows that this saying must have been particularly significant to early Christendom. Its old age is supported by the fact that in the song of love composed by the apostle Paul in the First Letter to the Corinthians we can recognize an allusion to this saying: "And if I have all faith, so as to remove mountains" (1 Cor. 13:2). Since in the contemporary environment there is no comparable turn of phrase that could have served as a model for an association of faith and moving mountains, this expression must go back to one of Jesus' sayings which has been transmitted by the Christian community.

It is not easy to decide which of the extant versions offers us the oldest form of the saying. Probably, however, it becomes visible behind the words of Mathew 17:20, since here there is talk about faith which can be as small as the tiny mustard seed. Jesus' parable of the mustard seed juxtaposes its excruciatingly small size with the stately plant that grows from it in order to illustrate, by means of this contrast, how wonderful the coming of God's reign will be (Mark 4:30-32, par). In Jesus' saying about the power of faith as well, the enormous effect which goes out from a very small stimulus is described. The folowing is then added as clarification, "and nothing will be impossible to you." With these words the evangelist contradicts the disciples' weak faith and points to the power of faith that trusts in the suffering, dying, and rising Son of man (Matt. 17:22 ff).

Such graphic language about moving mountains was very rare in Palestinian Judiasm and was customary in a quite different context. It could be used to refer to a scribe who was able to argue in an extraordinarily sharp manner and was thus called a "mountain-mover,"[62] but never in the Judaism of that period was faith described with this turn of phrase. In that sharply pointed formulation of Jesus' saying—that even an apparently small faith could move mountains—we find the same paradoxical manner of speech charactering some of his other words, for example the statement that it is "easier for a camel to go through the eye of a needle than for a rich man to enter the kingdom of God" (Mark 10:25, par). It can thus be assumed that Jesus' statement about faith is to be traced back to him, and did not emerge only later in the tradition of the Christian community.[63] The Christian community has a tendency to soften the challenging sharpness of Jesus' words or at least to make it more bearable. Jesus, however, emphasizes that whoever believes will be able to accomplish incredible things. God created the mountains by his word (Ps. 65:6; 90:2; and elsewhere), and at the end of time mountains are to be moved away and leveled (Isa. 40:4; 49:11; and elsewhere). Thus whoever is able to move mountains will participate in God's creative activity.[64]

The parallel to Jesus' saying transmitted in the Gospel of Luke also speaks in the conditional clause about faith as small as a mustard seed (Luke 17:6), but in the following clause it employs a different image than does the Matthean version: if faith were to speak to a sycamine tree that it should be uprooted and planted in the sea, it would obey. The sycamine tree thought of here was considered to be a particularly securely rooted tree, and one assumed it could stand in the earth for six hundred years.[65] Since Palestinian phrases are used in this image as well, we could have an independent parallel tradition before us which might be very old—since there are no parallels in the New Testament environment for this expression to which the graphic statement might be referred. In all probability, however, the older version of the saying is preserved in Matthew 17:20; and by means of the association made at an early stage in the transmission with the cursing of the fig tree (Mark 11:20-25), an alteration of the image from a mountain to a type of fig tree was made.[66]

The Markan version of the saying is influenced by the context into which the evangelist has placed it. Jesus and the disciples come by the fig tree, which has withered as a result of Jesus' curse. When Peter draws attention to the effect the curse had, Jesus says to the disciples, "Have faith in God" (Mark 11:22). This establishes the transition to Jesus' saying about faith. Faith is able to perform even greater miracles than the destruction of the tree just seen that had no fruit. The prerequisite, admittedly—and here something is expressed that was important to early Christian community instruction— is that there be no doubt in one's heart (cf James 1:6-8). Wherever in the power of faith one says to this mountain[67] that it should throw itself into the sea, it will happen. In the Markan version there is neither talk about faith in the conditional clause—only in the following clause do we read, "but believe"—nor is there a comparison with a mustard seed. Here it shows itself to be secondary when juxtaposed to the version of the saying-tradition, yet the paradoxical character of Jesus' words also is expressed here. Faith which does not place its trust in itself, but rather expects everything from God, is the strongest power. Whereas in Matthew 17:20 this faith is elevated above petty faith, in Mark faith is characterized as the opposite of every kind of doubt and is brought into the context of prayer that turns to God with full trust. This kind of prayer does not go unheard, but will rather receive fulfillment (Mark 11:24 ff).

Faith—and this idea lies at the base of the various versions of the saying—gains participation in God's power. With this characterization of faith Jesus picks up on the Old Testament prophetic understanding. Whoever believes stands on the ground laid by God himself. Wherever men are filled with this confident trust, they can effect what otherwise no person can.

3. Faith and Miracles

The Christian community took up this saying of Jesus about the unique power of faith and first expressed that this power of faith is awakened by the encounter with Jesus. Since Jesus had ascribed to faith the power to perform miracles, it was totally logical that the Christian community not only associated faith with prayer that receives an answer from trust in God, but also narratively portrayed the connection between faith and miracles. In doing this it used that manner of speech normally employed in the ancient world when one spoke about extraordinary occurrences, and it sought to portray Jesus of Nazareth as the one who triumphed over sickness and suffering and showed himself to be Lord of the powers of nature.

There are numerous parallels in the contemporary Palestinian and hellenistic traditions to the miracle stories told in the Gospels, parallels which deal with healings, exorcisms of demons, raisings from the dead, and peculiar natural occurrences. In a set narrative pattern one described how misery and death were overcome. First one told about the suffering of the sick person and the helplessness of the people around him. Against this background the miraculous event is then thrown even more splendidly into relief. The success that the miracle-worker wins through the exorcism of evil spirits or a victory over sickness is revealed before all eyes, and the astonished, reverent praise of those present confirms what happened. We have never before seen anything like it!

We often find talk about faith in the healing stories told by the Gospels. A necessary prerequisite for a miracle-worker's activity is everywhere the fact that he needs the trusting confidence of those who expect help from him. The rabbi or priest of some deity is sought out by people who do not know what to do and in their need turn to where they hope to acquire supernatural help. But neither in the healing stories recounted in the rabbinic tradition,[68] nor in the hellenistic miracle stories[69] is this posture called faith. In the Gospels, on the other hand, we repeatedly read, "Your faith has made you well" (Mark 5:34, par; 10:52, par; Luke 18:42; Luke 17:19).

According to Mark 5:34, parallel, Jesus is speaking to a hemorrhaging woman who had clung to him in her helplessness. "Go in peace"—he tells her—"and be healed of your disease." The evangelist Matthew adds, "And instantly the woman was made well" (9:22). This story tells about sickness and healing with characteristics typical of hellenistic miracle stories.[70] The author speaks about the length of the sickness (Mark 5:25, par) and about the futile employment of physicians (v 26) in order to show how virtually hopeless it appeared that she could ever be freed from her suffering. The healing, however, then happens by her touching Jesus, by which the power of recovery pours over her (vv 27-32, par). When Jesus remarks that healing power has gone out from him, and asks the surrounding crowd to tell him who has touched him (v 30, par), the scared woman admits the truth. Jesus, however, raises her up with the words about the saving power of faith. The portrayal's characteristics point unambiguously to the fact that it originated in the community tradition. That community, however, wants to emphasize that it was no healing gesture or the flowing of magically working power that conquered the sickness, but rather faith that turned to Jesus in full trust and received healing from him.

The same sentence "your faith has made you well" is used by the evangelist Mark in the story about the healing of the blind Bartimaeus (Mark 10:52, par; Luke 18:42).[71] He turns to Jesus with a plea for sight. Jesus answers his cry for help by telling him his faith has made him well. The effect of these words come about immediately. "And immediately he received his sight and followed him on the way (Mark 10:52, par). This

alludes to the fact that the saving faith leads one into following
Jesus. Jesus is going to Jerusalem and will suffer death (Mark
11–15, par). On his way to the cross he gives sight to a blind
person. Jerusalem, however, does not comprehend the
significance of the hour.

As a parallel to the story of the healing of the blind
Bartimaeus, the evangelist Matthew produces a story of two
blind people (9:27-31). Jesus asks them, "Do you believe that I
am able to do this?" (v 28). After they answer the question in the
affirmative he touches their eyes and says to them, "According
to your faith be it done to you" (v 29). The eyes of the blind men
are opened, and they are able to see.

The evangelist Luke takes up the passage about saving
faith again in a story that we find only in his Gospel. Of ten
lepers whom Jesus has healed, only one comes back to him
thankfully—and that is a Samaritan (17:11-19). To him is given
the word, "Rise and go your way; your faith has made you well"
(v 19). Whereas none of the Jews who were healed of leprosy
bring God the appropriate thanks, the person of foreign birth is
the only one who comes to Jesus as a believer.

The healing stories whose climax is the sentence "your
faith has made you well," received their present form from the
community that confessed the crucified and risen Christ as
Savior and Lord. It had the conviction that the faith which
knows of God's divinity makes demons tremble and wins
control of them (James 2:19). Christian exorcists could thus use
the phrase "your faith has made you well" in order to proclaim
the triumph of Christ over demons and disease.[72] This firm
association of the concepts "faith" and "saving" was familiar to
the community as part of Christian proclamation. The apostle
Paul can presuppose as universal Christian knowledge among
the Corinthians the sentence that believers experience saving
through acceptance of the gospel (1 Cor. 15:2; see p 98). The
early Christian confession emphasizes that faith in the risen
Lord is a saving faith (Rom. 10:9; see p 102), and Acts frequently

points to the saving power of faith (15:11; 16:31 ff). Through this believing turn to the Lord one receives help and simultaneously establishes the new life as a member of the community.

It is reported that Paul looked at the lame man he met in Lystra and saw "that he had faith to be made well," and thus he called to him in a loud voice that he should stand upright (Acts 14:9 ff). The lame man was immediately able to jump up and walk around. Faith in the name of the crucified and resurrected Christ gave the lame man healing and wholeness (cf Acts 3:16). Since this saving affects the entire person, the phrase "your faith has made you well" can be used in another context in Luke 7:50. Here it is not found in a miracle story, but is rather presented as the words Jesus speaks to a penitent sinner. Saving means forgiveness of sins and the opening of a new life.

The story of the hemorrhaging woman is closely associated with the raising of the daughter of the synagogue ruler Jairus (Mark 5:21-43). In the same crowd surrounding Jesus and the worried father we find this woman who clings to Jesus (v 34). The encounter between Jesus and the pleading father is interrupted by this scene. Meanwhile time has gone by and the sick girl dies. Her death is reported to the father with the remark that it is now useless to trouble the master. Jesus, however, overhears this and demands of the father: "Do not fear, only believe" (v 36). With this sentence the decisive word is spoken that simultaneously forms the connection with the preceding healing story. Only through faith that trusts Jesus is deliverance acquired. The raising of the dead girl is then described with phrases that again are characteristic of the style of miracle stories. The anxiety of the people concerned is heightened to the fullest (v 36); the lamenting crowd points out that nothing more can help against the power of death (vv 38-40a); the spectators are sent out (v 40b); words and gestures cause the awakening (v 41); the miracle immediately occurs (v 42) and is proven by the fact that the girl is given food (v 43). The narrative is structured in the same way as the typical miracle story of antiquity; the words about faith, however, give it the particular characteristic different from comparable contemporary accounts. It is not the action of a man gifted with divine power that effects the healing, but rather faith that saves because it trusts that God is acting in Jesus, and it does not let itself be led astray even in the face of death. This also supplies the contrasting element for the following story about Jesus' appearance in his home town Nazareth. Jesus performs no miraculous deeds there because he encounters no faith, but rather only unbelief (Mark 6:6). According to the story he laid his hands only on a few sick people and healed them (6:5).

The theme of faith also plays an important role in the story about the healing of the epileptic boy (Mark 9:14-29, par). Once again we encounter the typical characteristics of miracle stories of antiquity. The description of the sickness is given a great deal of space (vv 17 ff; 20;26); the miraculous healing is then thrown into even stronger relief (9:27). The father first turns to Jesus with the timid request for Jesus to have pity—if only he can help (v 22). Jesus picks the question up by repeating the words "if you can!" and adding: "All things are possible to him who believes" (v 23). This turn of phrase corresponds to the sentence, "For all things are possible with God" (Mark 10:27, par). This is why the pleading father's cry "I believe; help my unbelief!" is answered. His epileptic son is healed.

Faith implores Jesus and he grants its request. This connection between faith and prayer is particularly underscored by the evangelist Matthew.[73] He goes beyond the Markan version before him when he calls the Canaanite women's behavior faith. "Great is your faith! Be it done for you as you desire" (Matt. 15:28, par; Mark 7:29). This same phrase, which is typical for the evangelist, is found at the end of the story about the centurion of Capernaum which he, like Luke, took over from the tradition of sayings. The narrative he found before him already had something to say about faith, since Jesus says he had not yet found such faith in Israel (Matt. 8:10, par;

Luke 7:9).[74] The evangelist Matthew, however, expands the account with an additional saying. There he juxtaposes the sons of the kingdom, who will be thrown into the outer darkness, with the many who sit at the table with Abraham, Isaac, and Jacob (Matt. 8:11 ff, par; Luke 13:28-30). Only then comes the sentence that Jesus directs to the centurion at the end, again emphasizing the faith motif. "Go; be it done for you as you have believed" (Matt. 8:13). Afterward Jesus does not merely perform a powerful deed, but also answers the trusting plea of a faith that turns to him, grants it, and offers his help.

The faith spoken of in the miracle stories is not just precipitated by the miracle, but rather emerges from the encounter with Jesus. It thus precedes the miracle and puts its confidence in Jesus as the Savior.[75] With this emphasis on faith the evangelists are describing what Jesus' call to discipleship meant during the period of his public ministry. Jesus interpreted scripture authoritatively and taught what its word says here and now as God's statement and commandment. In this his appearance in several respects displayed many of the characteristics of the Jewish scribes who explained the books of the Law and prophets and who gathered a circle of students around them. But whereas with the rabbis a pupil could try for acceptance into the teacher's circle and was accepted after a test, Jesus went to many different people with the challenge, "Follow me" (Mark 1:16-20, par; 2:14, par; and elsewhere). Those addressed stood up, left everything they had, and followed Jesus; but where there was apprehension, it never came to actual discipleship (Matt. 10:17-31, par). Anyone who became the pupil of a scribe could be named a rabbi himself after the successful conclusion of a long, thorough course of study, could acquire the corresponding authority, and himself found a school. Jesus' disciples, however, always remained the pupils of the master who stands over against them as Lord (Matt. 23:7 ff). They follow his words and share his path as his pupils. Whoever follows Jesus and takes up his cross will suffer with Christ, but will receive from him the life that no one can ever take away (Mark 10:34-36, par).

Discipleship in Jesus means—this is what the gospel writers portray—believing in Jesus and wholly trusting him. Whoever hears the call in this way experiences the transforming power of faith along the path with Jesus. The evangelists thus emphasize this motif of the saving power of faith in the stories telling of the healing of the sick or of the deliverance of lost people. In this way the miracle stories become exemplary portrayals of faith, demonstrating its active power. While looking to Jesus one experiences deliverance and healing; but this also lays the foundation for the new life lived in his discipleship.

III. The Pauline Letters: Justification by Faith

1. By Faith Alone

The apostle Paul was initially an opponent of the Christian faith.[76] In his letters he often speaks about his Jewish past and his persecution of the Christian communities. In this context he mentions his origin in Judaism and emphasizes—not without a certain pride—that he is an Israelite, was circumcised as a baby on the eighth day, comes from the tribe of Benjamin, is a Hebrew of Hebrews, was a Pharisee who lived strictly according to the law and had lived in perfect accordance with the law (Phil. 3:5 ff). Thus if some people believe they can fall back on the advantages of their purely Jewish origins, he need not feel inferior to them at all. Paul is convinced he did justice to every requirement one could put to a Jew who lives according to the law.

These comments of Paul describe his pre-Christian past and show us that the Jew Paul did not groan under the burden placed upon men by the demands of the law. On the contrary, he had the feeling of being able to do perfect justice to the law. This consciousness corresponded perfectly to the beliefs of faithful Jews during this period, since they considered the law to be the gift of God by means of which he singled out the people of Israel. Basically it was considered possible to fulfill its many requirements; and with the help of the law men could attain the righteousness God demanded of them. The fact that God gave the law is thus understood as an expression of his love, since through that law he gave his people the possibility of performing good works and acquiring merit. Thus according to Jewish conviction, the law meant life, and without the law there is no life. Paul says he distinguished himself from those his own age by keeping the law with zealousness (Gal. 1:14), and for this reason he joined the movement of the Pharisees, who strove for conscientious interpretation of the law and its careful execution, and he contradicted those who doubted the law's singular dignity. His strict Jewish way of life thus had to lead to his becoming an opponent of the Christians.

The original community in Jerusalem had initially tried to remain within the context of Judaism. Acts reports that the disciples went to the temple daily (Acts 2:46). Apparently the early Christians took part in the temple cult (cf Matt. 5:23 ff) and also paid the temple tax which every Jew owed to the holy place (cf Matt. 17:24-27). The fact that one confessed Jesus as the Messiah did not necessarily have as its consequence that one broke with Judaism, since even the famous scribe Rabbi Akiba, who had welcomed the leader of the Jewish rebels as the promised son of the stars Bar Kochba (cf Num. 24:17-19), remained a respected teacher in Israel in spite of the failure of this messianic movement (A.D.132–135), which also brought on his own death. The only thing decisive for membership in Judaism is the recognition of the obligatory nature of the law. Various understandings of the question concerning the messianic age could and were permitted to be entertained. Thus the Christians did not have to be separate from Judaism when they still considered themselves to be bound to the law. A break had to occur only when this stance toward the law was called into question.

This dispute was first taken up by a hellenistic Jewish group which through its speaker Stephen criticized the temple and law (Acts 6:13). Since faith in the crucified and risen Christ receives salvation, the temple and law can no longer represent the path to that salvation. This sermon immediately prompted Stephen's presecution and martyrdom and caused his followers' departure from Jerusalem. The Palestinian Jewish-Christian part of the original community, which stood under the leadership of the Twelve, was in contrast able to remain in the city (Acts 8:1). This shows that the church's separation from Judaism had to be carried out within the context of the posture toward the law. This problem was first recognized by the circle around Stephen and then, during the following decades, was the bone of contention between Christians and Jews until their paths finally separated for good.

Paul the Jew was a decided opponent of those Christians who expressed critical opinions about the temple and law. While their messianic belief might still be accepted as a particular opinion within Judaism, the reason for his sharp opposition can be found in the fact that they took a critical stance toward the law, which issued from their confession of Christ. That is why Paul became a persecutor of the community (Gal. 1:13; Phil. 3:6; 1 Cor. 15:9). And among Christians it was said he wanted to destory the faith (Gal. 1:23).[77]

This man who was a zealot of the law was suddenly won over to the faith in the crucified Christ. In contrast to the broadly structured portrayal of Paul's conversion given later by Acts (9:1-29; 22:3-21; 26:9-20), the apostle himself speaks about this decisive moment in his life with only very few words: "But when he who had set me apart before I was born, and had called me through his grace, was pleased to reveal his Son to me, . . . I did not confer with flesh and blood" (Gal. 1:15 ff). Paul mentions the event through which he became a Christian only in a secondary clause.[78] He understands it as God's deed, to be traced back to his decision of grace, and describes his calling with unmistakable reference to the word of God which once came to the prophet Jeremiah: "Before I formed you in the womb I knew you, and before you were born I consecrated you; I appointed you a prophet to the nations" (Jer. 1:5).[79] God's call—Paul emphasizes this—came to him through the revelation of his son. That is to say, "I have seen Jesus our Lord" (1 Cor. 9:1), "He appeared also to me" (1 Cor. 15:8). This appearance changed his life at its very foundation: "But whatever gain I had, I counted as loss for the sake of Christ. Indeed I count everything as loss because of the surpassing worth of knowing Christ Jesus my Lord. For his sake I suffered the loss of all things, and count them as refuse, in order that I may gain Christ and be found in him, not having a righteousness of my own, based on the law, but that which is through faith in Christ, the righteousness from God that depends on faith" (Phil. 3:7-9).

In these sentences Paul employs an image from business life in which one figures up profit and loss. The apostle says this kind of figuring was changed totally from the time he became a Christian. He once considered it profit to be able to put his own accomplishments before God. Now, however, he must list all that in the loss column because it only takes him away from God. The only gain consists in having recognized Christ, and his life's path will be guided by this recognition from now on. "Not that I have already obtained this or am already perfect; but I press on to make it my own, because Christ Jesus has made me his own" (Phil. 3:12). Righteousness according to the law is thus also to be listed on the negative side of the ledger, a righteousness of which Paul had been proud; and only God's saving mercy can be counted as positive, mercy which has been revealed in Christ and can only be received through faith.

The great turn in his life, which had disclosed to him that decisive insight into the saving power of faith in the crucified and risen Christ, this same turn was for Paul also the commissioning to apostleship. God called him—he says—"in order that I might preach him among the Gentiles" (Gal. 1:16). He is to communicate to them the same insight which he won by faith in Christ: only through trust in the gospel does salvation come to those who accept this liberating message in faith. The alternatives, law or Christ which those Christians had raised is thus taken up by Paul as the decisive question.

This theme can be elucidated by an occurrence the apostle recounts in the Letter to the Galatians (2:11-14). In the large city of Antioch a Christian community had emerged very early, to which former Jews as well as former Gentiles belonged. As Christians they realized they were bound to a single community and thus took common meals together. A pious Jew, however, could sit at a table with others only if they too kept the law's food and purity requirements. Thus when in Antioch former Jews got beyond these considerations and ate together with former Gentiles, they had gained the insight that the common faith in Christ was binding them together and that the earlier segregation was no longer valid. This understanding was also shared by Peter, whom Paul mentions here by his Aramaic name Cephas. But then suddenly people appeared in Antioch who were sent by James, the leader of the original Jerusalem community. In Jerusalem people were judging the developments in the Antioch community critically, since whenever Jewish Christians shared a table with Gentile Christians, they lost the possibility of keeping the company of Jews, for this has to be conducted according to the rules of the law. In that case, however, the dialogue with the Jews could no longer be carried on. It thus becomes clear why those in Jerusalem expressed concern regarding the behavior of the community in Antioch. Their arguments made a great impression and caused Peter—also Barnabas, who had been working with Paul—to give up sharing tables with the Gentile Christians and to withdraw again to the community of Jews and Jewish Christians. The consequences of this behavior, however, had to be that Gentile Christians were only able to continue eating commonly with Jewish Christians if they were willing to accept the law's requirement for themselves as well.

When Paul heard of these events, he disputed publicly with Peter and demanded an explanation from him; if one wanted to demand of Gentile Christians that they recognize the requirements of the law as a condition for participation in the functions of the community, then one would be forcing them to live like Jews. They would then have to become Jews in order to continue being around Jewish Christians. That, however, would be a betrayal of the truth of the gospel, since the only possible conclusion to be drawn from the preaching of Christ must be that Jews and Gentiles receive salvation only through the faith in Christ. The apostle mentions this occurrence in order clearly to show the Galatian community what one can learn from it. After Paul's departure, teachers had appeared in those communities in Asia Minor who wanted to persuade them that they would have to follow the law of Israel if they really wanted to fulfill God's will. They asserted that Paul had not told the whole truth to them as former Gentiles. To be sure, he had spoken about faith in Christ, but he had withheld from them the fact that one must take obedience to the law along with that faith in order to become heirs of the promises found in scripture. Paul turns against this teaching with unyielding decisiveness, because after God announced his mercy through Christ, from the Christian perspective the law can no longer open the way to salvation.

Paul adds a few sentences of fundamental reflection to the account of the occurrence in Antioch. He keeps using the form of address which turns to Peter and is to point out to him the dangerous inconsistency of his behavior (Gal. 2:15-21). No doubt—he says—we had the advantage of being Jews by nature and not Gentiles. But how did we become Christians? Certainly not by performing better and greater works as the Law demands and as every pious Jew might do. Our existence as Christians came rather only by our winning faith in Christ. This faith, however, implies the knowledge that God's mercy was revealed only on the cross of Christ. It is preached in the gospel and accepted by faith.

Paul's understanding of faith here joins with the Christendom which was already there before him and which had brought the content of faith to expression in short formulations (see pp 96 ff). The apostle did not first have to create a Christian theology from scratch, but rather found a theology already available in the statements of the early Christian confession, and he carried it on in his own turn.[80] He takes up their statements, assimilates them and draws the conclusions for the life of Christians. Whoever has received salvation through faith in Christ stands in the proper relationship to God. Works and deeds, as the law demands them, can never open the way to salvation. "For I," Paul says, "through the law died to the law" (Gal. 2:19). By this he means to say: Christ was nailed to the cross because the law brought him there. We, however, who belong to Christ, are crucified with him and thus also have died to the law with him, so that we can now say, "It is no longer I who live, but Christ who lives in me; and the life I now live in the flesh I live by faith in the Son of God, who loved me and gave himself for me" (Gal. 2:20).

The apostle calls on the Old Testament to justify this argument, and in so doing refers to a passage from Psalm 143. "For no man living is righteous before thee." Paul adds a polemical edge to the sentence by inserting the words "by works of the law" and saying that "no human being will be justified in his sight" (Rom. 3:20). It is beyond man's capacity to put himself into the correct relationship to God. The deeds performed in obedience to the requirements of the law can never bring man to an understanding of the meaning of his life. This can only be received as a gift from God. Thus the thesis won from this disputation reads as follows: "For we hold that a man is justified by faith apart from works of law" (Rom. 3:28).

In the Letter to the Romans Paul refers to an early Christian confessional statement that speaks of the salvation meaning of Christ's death.[81] "God put forward Christ Jesus as an expiation by his blood to show God's righteousness because in his divine forbearance he had passed over former sins" (Rom. 3:25 ff). This extremely compact statement—which is presumably taken out of a larger context—speaks in cultic and legal terms about the incomparable significance of Christ's death on the cross. His death is designated as a sacrifice of expiation that is effective by means of the spilled blood. And it is interpreted as proof of divine righteousness, which consists in nothing other than the mercy in which God was patient and now forgives sins for Christ's sake. Paul has taken up this sentence and inserted the words "by faith" between the words "expiation" and "by his blood," which belong together. With this emphatic remark he underscores that only in faith can that proof of God's righteousness be comprehended and accepted.

2. Abraham the Father of Believers

Paul understands full well that for readers of the Old Testament he must demonstrate the persuasive power of this thesis in a story that speaks in an exemplary fashion of divine righteousness and man's faith. Abraham was considered by all Jews to be the model of the pious person. Although he lived long before the time of Moses, and although consequently the law, which was given to Israel at Sinai, was not yet available, according to Jewish tradition he already knew God's whole will and kept it in all its aspects. But how did Abraham do what God wanted of him, through the works with which he did what the law demands or through the faith with which he put his trust in God?

In contemporary Judaism there was continual discussion concerning what kind of righteousness it was which God reckoned to Abraham. He also remained obedient in the hour of his most difficult temptation, when his son was demanded of him. He was—so we read in the First Book of Maccabees, which was composed shortly after 100 B.C.—"found faithful when tested, and it was reckoned to him as righteousness" (1 Macc. 2:52).

Abraham's praise is sung in the sayings of Jesus Sirach:

Abraham was the great father of a multitude of nations,
    and no one has been found like him in glory;
he kept the law of the Most High,
    and was taken into covenant with him;
he established the covenant in his flesh,
    and when he was tested he was found faithful.
Therefore the Lord assured him by an oath
    that the nations would be blessed through his posterity;
that he would multiply him like the dust of the earth,
    and exalt his posterity like the stars,
and cause them to inherit from sea to sea
    and from the River to the ends of the earth.
                                        (Ecclus. 44:19-21)

Jewish understanding considered Abraham's life to be evidence of the loyalty to the law with which he performed the deeds suitable for a person who respects God's law and lives according to it. Reckoning his actions as righteousness means that the proper behavior demanded and rendered possible by the law emerges from the sum of his deeds.[82] His faith represents one element of merit among others which he can present to God.

They are noted in his favor and recognized by God, so that the ledger of guilt and merit shows a positive balance. Philo of Alexandria considered Abraham's faith to be the crowning of the pious life in which he came to the full recognition that God alone is enduring reality. Abraham was, "as they say, the first who believed in God and who as the first one had an unchangeable and secure conviction that there is an ultimate cause and that it takes care of the world and what is in it."[83] Abraham acquired this insight from an observation of the world whose meaningful unity he understood as God's creation; he had lifted his eyes above heaven and the stars until he gained a clear understanding of God's existence and providence.[84]

The apostle Paul pushes aside the form the Abraham narrative had received in the Jewish tradition as well as the hellenistic reinterpretation as represented by Philo of Alexandria; in Galatians (3:1–5:12) and Romans (ch 4) he then reaches directly back to scripture.[85] His argument revolves around the decisive sentence, "Abraham believed the Lord; and he reckoned it to him as righteousness" (Gen. 15:6; Gal. 3:6; Rom. 4:3). With reference to this scriptural passage Paul explains what Abraham's faith means. Abraham trusted in God's promise from faith and thus made space for God's controlling actions. He placed himself in the only proper relationship to God that can be designated as righteousness because he held God's promise to be more real than anything else he could see.[86] With this statement Paul is contradicting the Jewish interpretation, according to which the patriarch's faith was judged to be meritorious and could be listed alongside other deeds of obedience. Whereas the rabbis never doubted that Abraham received justification from works, Paul refers to the statement in scripture and maintains that Abraham was justified before God only through faith.

The polemical limitations brought forth here are expounded in the Letter to the Galatians with particular sharpness and are developed within the context of the Old

Testament. One reads there that Abraham was blessed through God's promise and that this blessing itself was then promised, through Abraham, to the nations (Gal. 3:8). The law, on the other hand, demands deeds, and curses all those who do not fulfill the requirements of the law (Gal. 3:10). Since God's blessing can never be attained by the deeds man is able to perform under his own power, only he who through faith stands in the only proper relationship to God will receive life (Gal. 3:11). The law puts us under a curse; Christ, however, redeemed us from the curse—as Paul explains with reference to Deuteronomy 21:23. There one reads that the corpse of an executed person is to be hung on a tree and is to remain there until the evening as a sign of the curse spoken over him. Paul refers this sentence to the crucified Christ and concludes that Christ took up the curse of the law upon himself and removed it (Gal. 3:13 ff). But that then clears the way for the promises given to Abraham and his seed (ie, his posterity) to come to those who are to receive them: "And if you are Christ's, then you are Abraham's offspring, heirs according to promise" (Gal. 3:29).

Paul does not understand Abraham's faith as a past event that transpired long ago. Abraham appears to him rather as the model of the kind of faith now alive in the Christian community, which puts its trust in the gospel of the crucified and risen Christ. One might, of course, raise doubts by mentioning that Abraham was only able to know the promise, while the Christians have experienced its fulfillment.[87] But as acutely conscious as Paul is of the temporal distance between the Christians and their father Abraham, he nonetheless says unequivocally that Abraham's faith is not qualitatively different from that of the Christians. The promise to which Abraham clung is virtually identical with the gospel; Abraham's faith, after all, trusts only in the word of God spoken to him just as does the faith of the Christians. Faith does not grow from seeing, and certainly not from some compelling proof, but only from the power of the word which faith knows is addressing it. This is why Paul maintains expressly that the statement about Abraham's faith-righteousness was not just written for his sake, "but for ours also. It will be reckoned to us who believe in him that raised from the dead Jesus our Lord, who was put to death for our trespasses and raised for our justification" (Rom. 4:23-25).

This faith does not deceive itself concerning the reality around it, and does not create illusions. On the contrary, Abraham saw with perfect clarity what was standing in the way of God's promise of a son. He looked at his own aged body and remained aware of the fact that for Sarah the time was long past when she could have become a mother (Rom. 4:19). Nonetheless he did not become weak in faith, but rather trusted in the promise that said he was to become the father of many nations (Rom. 4:18). Abraham believed in the God "who gives life to the dead and calls into existence the things that do not exist" (Rom. 4:17). Whereas Jewish statements also speak about the God who gives life to the dead,[88] Paul includes the sentence in the confession that God has revealed who he is through the resurrection of Jesus Christ from the dead—the same who in the beginning spoke to things that did not exist that they were to be. From this confidence faith gains the power to hope against all appearances, even where apparently there is nothing to hope.

When Abraham trusted in faith in God's promise, the law was not yet available. Furthermore, Abraham had at that time not yet received the sign of the covenant, circumcision; but was rather uncircumcised like the Gentiles (4:10 ff). From this one can conclude that circumcision only came later, as a seal on righteousness by faith—but it did not create that righteousness. Thus Abraham remains the father of believers to whom—like him—faith is reckoned as righteousness. They step into his footsteps as sons (Rom. 4:12).

Faith is free from any appearance of self-praise, and rather represents its complete opposite. Whenever a person shows his deeds and claims merit for his works, there he can rightfully ask for recognition (Rom. 4:4 ff). That is the sense in which Jewish tradition interpreted Abraham's behavior, which was considered to be the model of a pious life. "Thus you will find," the Midrash explains,[89] "that our father Abraham took possession of this and the future world only through the merit of faith with which he believed in the Lord, as it is written: He believed in the Lord and he reckoned it to him as righteousness." Paul counters this understanding by pointing out that Abraham believed the word of God before the coming of the law, which proves that the promise went to him as the father of believers alone through the power of faith righteousness (Rom. 4:13). That is why the Christian community claims him as their father, to whom they belong as heirs of the promise (Rom. 4:1).

Paul remained puzzled that Israel, as the chosen people of God, did not open itself up to the faith in Christ. The apostle dealt extensively with this problem and struggled for a solution (Rom. 9–11). He would have been willing to be cursed and separated from Christ for the sake of his people, if in that way his brethren would come to Christ (9:3). He gives a three-fold answer to the pressing question of why they are persisting in unbelief. The first points to God's election and rejecting: the God who is merciful to those to whom he shows mercy and compassionate to those to whom he shows compassion (9:6-29). The rejection of Christ by Israel can thus be traced back to God's inscrutable decision by which he has created a schism in his people. Thus not all who come from Israel are really Israel. Only the children of the promise are counted as its progeny. Thus God's own free choice has caused Israel's stubbornness.

After this first train of thought Paul begins again and gives a second answer to the question concerning Israel's rejection of the gospel (9:30–10:21). Its unbelief is and remains its own fault, and it alone is responsible for it. The Gentiles, who have not striven for righteousness, attained the righteousness that comes from faith. Israel, however, which chased after the righteousness of the law, missed the mark, since it wanted to build righteousness from works, as the law demands. Because they wanted to erect their own righteousness, they are not subject to the righteousness of God (10:3). The path they traveled, however, can never lead to righteousness, since Christ is the end of the law, and only he who believes in him will receive righteousness. Faith, however, comes from preaching, so the apostle takes up the prophetic lament, "Lord, who has believed what he has heard from us?" (10:16). Israel has hardened itself against the proclamation, but God's loyalty continues to hold forth the invitation and awaits the homecoming of his people.

After Paul contrasts both statements to each other—God's election and Israel's disobedience—he then, in a third section, expresses the confidence that God does not regret his gifts and election (11:1-32). That means Israel's history has not yet reached its conclusion. Since God's pronouncements and promises do not depend on human behavior, Israel, too, will be saved. The apostle trusts in the fact that, like the Gentiles, the Jews will also receive and accept salvation through faith, since God has included everyone among the unbelievers so that everyone can receive his mercy. Both Jews and Gentiles will thus experience God's compassion precisely through the justification of the godless. His mercy stands at the end of all the paths down which he leads his people.

Even if Israel and Christendom are separated by their different answers to the gospel, they are nonetheless joined precisely by that which separates them. They have in common the inheritance and promises of their fathers, indeed the emergence of Christ from his people (Rom. 9:4 ff). According to the apostle's conviction, God will one day join their paths together again so that they can together praise the richness of God's wisdom (11:33-36). [90]

3. The Life of the Believers

Faith arises from the affirming acceptance of the Christian proclamation, an acceptance standing at the beginning of being a Christian.[91] Paul repeatedly speaks about the fact that the members of the community have come to faith (1 Cor. 15:2; Rom. 13:11; and elsewhere). This refers to the initial phase establishing membership in the community, and the apostle sometimes talks about this process of becoming a Christian by referring to having become a believer, and sometimes by referring to baptism (1 Cor. 1:13 ff; 6:11; Rom. 6:1-14; and elsewhere). If he speaks about Christians having become believers, then he reminds the reader they have spoken this yes as an answer to the proclaimed gospel; and if he refers to baptism, he emphasizes that God's merciful act laid the foundation of their Christian existence. Both statements describe one and the same occurrence establishing firm membership in the Body of Christ, and they thus form a unity. The sinner's justification, acquired in baptism, is itself acquired by the answer of faith. Thus in Galatians 3:26 ff, when Paul explains membership in Christ with the statement, "For as many of you as were baptized into Christ have put on Christ," then it follows logically for him that those belonging to Christ are the heirs of Abraham (Gal. 3:29). Abraham's sons, however—this is what the entire chapter 3 has intended to show (see p 103 above)—are not those associated with him through lineage and law, but rather "it is men of faith who are the sons of Abraham" (3:7). They have received God's spirit, which grants new life. Paul thus reminds the Galatians of this foundation of their Christian existence by asking them how they began (3:2 ff)—not in works of the law, but rather with the spirit of God, bequeathed in baptism, and with faith, which received God's act as the foundation and power of the new life in Christ. That membership in Christ, acquired in baptism, is thus assimilated in the confessing faith of the person baptized.[92]

The gospel—this is how the apostle emphasizes it in the fundamental theme at the beginning of the Letter to the Romans—"is the power of God for salvation to every one who has faith, to the Jew first and also to the Greek. For in it the righteousness of God is revealed through faith for faith; as it is written, 'He who through faith is righteous shall live' " (1:16 ff). God's power is activated in the seemingly foolish word of the cross for the deliverance of all believers, since in its proclamation God's righteousness is revealed, which as his gift can only be taken up in faith. Anyone accepting this message relinquishes any self-praise or the possibility of wanting to assert oneself with the help of the law, and from now on lives in faith in Christ. Faith answering to the gospel can thus also be called obedience by Paul (Rom. 1:5; 10:16; 16:19; and elsewhere), since an affirming posture necessarily results in the gospel itself determining the believer's life and action from then on. Thus Paul can also describe Christian existence with expressions such as "having faith" (Rom. 14:22; Philem. 5), "being in faith" (2 Cor. 13:5), "standing in faith" (1 Cor. 16:13; 2 Cor. 1:24), or similar phrases such as "standing in the Lord," (1 Thes. 3:8), "standing in grace" (Rom. 5:2), or "standing in the gospel" (1 Cor. 15:1).[93] Paul shows here that the affirming acceptance of the gospel does not just represent a one-time act which takes place at the beginning of being a Christian; that faith which stands at the beginning needs rather to be sustained in the entire life of the Christian. The Christian belongs to his Lord and is to follow him in all areas of life; after all, his "old person" is crucified with Christ and now Christ lives in him (Gal. 2:20). Thus the powers and forces that previously held sway over him can no longer make any claims on him. The person can never belong only to himself, but is rather perpetually subject to a lord. If he thinks he is able to maintain control over himself, then he inevitably falls prey to the slavery of sin, law, and death, which have set up their rule in this world

(Rom. 7:7-25). The Christian, however, knows that these forces can no longer make that claim on him, since their reign is broken with the baptism into Christ's death. This, however, establishes the believers' new way of life to be carried out in discipleship (Rom. 6:1-4), since "if we have died with Christ, we believe that we shall also live with him" (Rom. 6:8).

Faith is thus not only related to the past—to the event of cross and resurrection of Christ—but simultaneously to the future, which joins its life to that of Christ. It is in hope that faith focuses on the fulfillment of the pronouncement made to it. In doing this, hope grounds itself—as the example of Abraham shows—on nothing other than God's pronouncement itself. It does not rest on external appearances, and it is also maintained in the face of all criticism and doubt, since God's pronouncement is considered more real than anything that can be seized and held. Thus Abraham "believed in hope against hope" (Rom 4:18). He went contrary to that hope known to men and based his trust alone in the hope which itself trusts in God's promise. Martin Luther, in the lectures he gave in 1515–16 on the Letter to the Romans, described the nature of this hope grounded in faith by distinguishing it from the other hope, which directs itself to those things one can normally hope for. "What men hope for is not against hope, but rather commensurate with it, that is: it is quite possible it may come to pass. Men do not hope when the opposite of what they hope for stands before them, but rather only when something is similar to it or if a firm possibility exists that what is hoped for can come to pass. Thus this hope is more against than for the Christian hope, since one confidently expects that future thing one hopes for only if one has its secure beginning in hand. Only then does one hope that no more obstacles get in the way of what one hopes for. If one is to affirm that hope, then one also wants to be sure and have reliable information; but where there is no security, hope must remain uncertain. Christian hope is, however, certain in a pure no, since it knows that what one hopes for must come and cannot be detained, because no one can detain God. But it is uncertain concerning what is present now, since here it has no supports of any kind in which it can place its trust. That for which it hopes is much too hidden; only its opposite is revealed. That is why the (Christian) hope is more a yes than a no." This is why "faith is a steep and difficult thing."[94]

Faith, whose hope is not based on what is visible, but rather on what one cannot comprehend (Rom. 8;24 ff), knows that it has not yet reached its goal, so it stretches out toward the future which will bring fulfillment (Gal. 5:5). Paul is far removed from the opinion that faith could or might remain by itself or find satisfaction only in itself. He decisively maintains that only through faith and never through works of the law can righteousness be attained (Rom. 9:30–10:3); but the apostle emphasizes with equal decisiveness that the faith which determines the believers' entire life must be manifested in love (Gal. 5:6). In this, however, it is not subject to a law giving it a list of demands it must fulfill. The believers are rather called to freedom through Christ (Gal. 5:1; 13). This freedom, however, binds them to the task of serving one another in love. A person justified through faith in Christ; that is, a person accepted by God, is by no means released into the boundless freedom of the enthusiast who thinks he can do or not do what pleases him. He is "not without law," but rather "stands under the law of Christ" (1 Cor. 9:21). He encounters his neighbor in love that carries the other person's burdens and thus fulfills the law of Christ (Gal. 6:2). This is how God's will finds its real, original fulfillment (Rom. 13:8). All the commandments, after all, are contained in the one, "You shall love your neighbor as yourself" (Rom. 13:9; Gal. 5:14).

For Paul the phrase "through faith" means nothing other than "by grace" (Rom. 4:16). "Under grace," however, represents the complete opposite of "under the law" (Rom. 6:14). Living from God's offer of grace means that henceforth sin no longer has a claim to power, since the believers do not yield their members to sin as instruments of wickedness, but rather to God as instruments of righteousness (Rom. 6:13). Their way of life stands under the power of Christ, whom believers praise through their confessing word and the act of love. They are liberated from the necessity of having to prove their righteousness through achievements, as the law demands. But that also frees them for the undivided service of love in which the one is there for the other. Just as faith shows itself as hope, so also is it active through love. If Christian existence can be described as faith, love, and hope, then love is the greatest of these three (1 Cor. 13:13), since hope will one day find fulfillment and faith be changed into seeing; love, however, remains. "Love bears all things, believes all things, hopes all things, endures all things" (1 Cor. 13:7).

Faith in the crucified and risen Christ, which trusts absolutely in the assurance of God's mercy, cannot be separated from its content. Thus it cannot be adequately described as the expression of a new self-understanding, according to which man decides against establishing himself solely through his own powers and understands himself before God rather as one who has received a radical bequest.[95] This new self-understanding retains its foundation and point of reference rather in the pronouncement of the message of Christ. Just as do the authors in the Old Testament, Paul also understands faith as a trusting in something which is recognized as valid and certain. But he attributes this confidence only to the manifestation of God's grace, which took place on the cross of Christ and is promised by the gospel. Faith thus does not give deliverance because it opens up a new self-understanding to man, but because it is the faith in Christ Jesus.[96]

IV. Faith Within the Life of the Church

1. The Post-Pauline Letters: Correct Faith

Christendom in the second and third generations always remained aware that the life of Christians is carried by faith. It is not based on sense perception, but rather on the proclaimed gospel, since the members of the community believe in Christ even though they have not seen him (1 Peter 1:8). Faith directs itself toward the future in which its lasting inheritance is to be revealed (1 Peter 1:4 ff), and for that reason it must suffer various trials (1 Peter 1:6 ff) and maintain itself against the deceptive attacks of the devil (1 Peter 5:9).

But how can faith be preserved in these spiritual struggles to which Christians are subjected? The emerging church tried to determine more precisely how the content of faith might be secured and protected against falsification, so it coined the term "correct faith" and differentiated it from false faith. This gave the discussion of faith a pedagogical coloring, which at the same time was supposed to protect its understanding against misinterpretation. In the Pastoral Letters, a product of the Pauline school around the turn of the first and second centuries, faith is understood primarily as doctrine which the church is to preserve in its true form. When the mystery of faith is discussed there (1 Tim. 3:9), the writer employs rigidly formulated phrases from the christological confession. Of Christ it is said, "He was manifested in the flesh, vindicated in the Spirit, seen by angels, preached among the nations, believed in the world, taken up in glory" (1 Tim. 3:16). The content of faith is secured in the correct doctrine and passed on in the community (1 Tim. 4:6). In reverse fashion, whoever gives up faith falls prey to false doctrine (1 Tim. 4:1). The false teachers "have made shipwreck of their faith" (1 Tim. 1:19; 6:21) and as a result have not proven themselves in faith (2 Tim. 3:8).[97] They are a danger to the community because they pervert the faith of others by their talk and behavior (2 Tim. 2:18). Thus it is important "to be sound in faith" (Titus 1:13; 2:2) and to secure or recover it when it is threatened. Whoever relies on "sound doctrine" (1 Tim. 1:10; 2 Tim. 4:3; Titus 1:9; 2:1) as it is offered by the officials of the church, will be protected from seduction and will know how to defend himself against the whisperings of false teachers.

Those false teachers, on the other hand, who have forsaken correct faith, represent a different doctrine (1 Tim. 1:3; 6:3) which not only distorts the meaning of faith's content, but also leads one astray into a looser life-style. In the face of all these disputes, which only vaguely describe the position of the opposition, all emphasis is placed upon the community's not being lost in faith (1 Tim. 1:2, 4; Titus 3:15; and elsewhere). In this process, the use of the word faith—which in part takes on a formal, polished coloring—almost assumes the meaning that the word Christianity had later on. And if it is true that one must by all means remain true to correct faith, then that faith must be discernable in the correct behavior of Christians. Thus the Pauline thesis that salvation is received only through faith recedes into the background.

To be sure, the Pastoral Letters display a whole series of genuinely Pauline formulations; we hear about God's mercy on sinners, among whom Paul is the foremost (1 Tim. 1:12 ff), about justifications not from works (Titus 3:5), and about the appearance of the saving grace of God in Christ (2 Tim. 1:10 ff; Titus 2:11 ff; 3:4 ff). This Pauline theology, however, has been further developed by a continuing school of tradition. Thus these Pastoral Letters do not coin any new christological statements, but rather take over exclusively preformulated phrases that describe Christ as the mediator between God and men who has given himself as the ransom for all men (1 Tim. 2:5 ff).[98] Faith, however, which is so strongly emphasized in Pauline theology, has become correct faith in the Pastoral Letters, and is listed as one virtue among other Christian virtues (1 Tim. 4:12). Since faith thus forfeits its central significance, it is no wonder that the demand for good works can be raised again unaffectedly, since they prove that God's grace has prepared and equipped the members of the community for new life (1 Tim. 2:10; 5:10; 6:18; 1 Tim. 2:21; 3:17). Christ gave himself—this is how the goal of Christ's work is described—"to redeem us from all iniquity and to purify for himself a people of his own who are zealous for good deeds" (Titus 2:14). Thus the church, as the pillar and bulwark of the truth (1 Tim. 3:15; 2 Tim. 2:19), carries the responsibility for proclaiming and teaching God's revelation in Christ in the correct manner. Tradition is accordingly valued very highly, and the recipients of the letters are told to guard this entrusted gift with care (1 Tim. 6:20; 2 Tim. 1:12, 14; 2:2).

If, as in Ephesians 4:5, the sequence "one Lord, one faith, one baptism" refers to the one faith to which the communities are to cling with unwavering constancy, then its pedagogical and doctrinal form as offered by the church is understood in the latest New Testament writings from the beginning of the second century as a guide to the correct confession. That "most holy faith" (Jude 20), as it was "once for all delivered to the saints," joins the members of the community together in the correctly believing church, members "who have obtained a faith of equal standing with ours" (2 Peter 1:1).

2. The Letter of James: Faith and Works

In the Letter of James, put together as a collection of sayings toward the end of the first century, there is a discussion

concerning the relationship between faith and works which is to
be understood as a guide to correct Christian behavior (James
2:14-26).[99] First the topic is presented which is to be treated:
Faith without works cannot save one (before God). Then it is
shown that people in need cannot be helped with good
intentions, but rather only by means of acts of love. One can
thus say: Faith by itself, if it has no works, is dead (v 17). In a
second demonstration the author goes on to reach the same
conclusion, that faith without works is dead (v 26), and to
present this conclusion as irrefutable.

In a manner similar to more popular philosophical
presentations, the author of the letter first presents the
objections of an unnamed opponent who advocates the
separation of faith and works (v 18a). This objection, however,
is only presented as a backdrop against which the author's own
opinion can be developed more pointedly. Thus this is not a
clearly discernible false teaching with which one can carry on a
dispute, but rather a literary stylistic device enabling one's own
thesis to emerge all the more clearly. The objection is rejected
by showing that faith alone in the one God can by no means offer
saving power (v 19). When faith in the one God is mentioned in
this context, one should recognize that this is spoken within the
continuation of Jewish tradition, in which one daily speaks the
confession to the God of Israel. The Letter of James, which in
another passage knows very well how to say that Jesus Christ is
the content of faith (2:1), employs precisely this monotheistic
formulation here because it wants to point out that even the
demons believe in the one God—and shudder.[100] But precisely
here, in the fact that even the demons believe in the one God,
one sees the nullity of faith by itself. One must admittedly point
out here, however, that the Letter of James does not itself offer
any precise definition of faith. The letter is not concerned with a
dispute about correct or false faith; its center of gravity lies
rather in the question concerning the relationship between
faith and works.

After this negative delimitation the letter then shows positively that faith and works should work together in the life of the Christian. The example of Abraham serves here as an explanatory and confirming proof from scripture. Abraham was justified on the basis of his works, since he brought his son Isaac as a sacrifice to God. This fulfilled in Abraham's life what Genesis 15:6 had said of him, "And he believed the Lord; and he reckoned it to him as righteousness." In the most difficult of all the temptations Abraham had to withstand, he remained obedient. Thus from the beginning (Gen. 15) to the end (Gen. 22), faith and works acted together in Abraham. God recognized as righteous him who proved himself obedient to God's directions. Indeed, he was called the friend of God.

This understanding of Abraham's faith and works picks up on the Jewish evaluation of the patriarch (see above pp 128 ff). His fear of the Lord manifested itself in his obedience, so that he can serve virtually as a prototype of all those who preserve God's law unharmed in spite of temptations and trials. But while in the customary Jewish interpretation of Abraham's story the works were considered to be the most important element, to which faith was then also added as one among other good deeds, in the argument of the Letter of James, faith and works stand next to each other as equals. They are by no means permitted to be separated, but rather work together so that perfection in righteousness may be attained (2:22). Thus in the Letter of James we find an ethical motivation that, although coming from a Jewish heritage, nonetheless presupposes recognizable Christian concerns. Faith is to manifest itself in deeds and thereby lead to the creation of Christian perfection and righteousness.

At this point a significant contradition to Pauline theology emerges, since unlike the Letter of James, Paul's writing refers the example of Abraham exclusively to the saving power of faith (see above pp 129 ff). Abraham believed in the God who justifies the ungodly (Rom. 4:5). This faith—and not works of the law to which deserved wages must be paid—was reckoned to him as righteousness. The question thus arises, what is the relationship between the interpretations of the Abraham example by Paul and James?[101]

The author of the Letter of James is apparently not at all familiar with the particulars of Pauline theology; the letter has no precise definition of faith by which one might determine that it was directed against the Pauline understanding of faith, nor is it possible to maintain, for example, that Paul had freed faith from any obligation of performing works of active love (cf Gal. 5:6). One can thus assume that the author of the Letter of James only had certain misunderstood catch-phrases before him more than a generation after Paul. Weak allusions to Pauline formulations can be recognized only vaguely in phrases such as "without works" (without adding "of the law") "from faith alone," as well as the mention of the saving power of faith. The words of the apostle Paul have already hardened into pale formulas. Their real meaning has been forgotten almost as completely as the difficult struggle Paul once had to wage for the continued validity of the law or its end in Christ (see above pp 124 ff). Hence one cannot really speak of a direct polemic against Paul in the Letter of James. Its author seeks rather—notwithstanding a few catch-phrases which sound Pauline—to develop his thesis that faith and works can only together lead to perfection.

To be sure, Paul emphasizes (just as does the Letter of James) that faith must be active, but he would never admit that faith and works in conjunction with one another lead to righteousness. At this point Luther's justified criticism sets in: The Letter of James, completely at odds with Paul and all other scripture, grants justification to works; it wants to effect with works of the law what the apostles attain by means of encouragement to love.[102] The short Letter of James cannot, however, be considered as an actual antipode to Paul, since it contains no development of the original preaching of Christ. It offers rather a bundle of ethical admonitions that are to help the Christian attain righteousness. Thus not without reason does it stand on the periphery of the canon of New Testament writings, since its goal is a limited and modest one: To offer guidance and admonitions for a life pleasing to God. Even though one must side with Paul against the Letter of James and assert that righteousness is not gained by works, but rather received alone from faith, nonetheless it gives the Christian the task of being active in love and of assuming responsibility for others.[103] "After we are justified by faith," Luther says in his great lecture on the Letter to the Galatians, "we turn our attention to an active life."[104]

3. The Letter to the Hebrews: Faith as Steadfastness

In the Letter to the Hebrews the attempt is made to define the term faith: "Now faith is the assurance of things hoped for, the conviction of things not seen" (11:1). In this sentence, the unknown theologian who composed the letter does not go into the content of faith, but wants rather to emphasize its particular confidence and unshakable trust. Thus there is no complete description of faith given, but rather the reader's attention is directed to its fundamental characteristics. The Letter to the Hebrews would like to show a troubled congregation, in which doubt and insecurity were threatening to break out, that it is a matter of persevering loyally and of remaining with the community of God's people. That is why he emphasizes the steadfastness of faith, which is conscious of not yet having reached its goal and so yearns toward the future completion of salvation. Faith does not draw energy from the realm of tangible appearances, but lives rather from the world of that which is invisible, though no less real. It is convinced of the validity of the pronouncement of God given it and knows itself to be overcome by God's power, which remains invisible, but still gives faith strength through its word.[105]

This motif is taken up again and again in a long series of examples from Israel's history which vividly portray the conduct of faith (ch 11). In the sermon of the hellenistic synagogue similar sketches of Israel's history were variously employed, just as they were also used in early Christian instruction (cf Acts 7). The author of the Letter to the Hebrews placed his exemplary collection under the heading of faith, although in most of the Old Testament stories he uses it is not even mentioned. In his section dealing with Abraham, nonetheless, he peculiarly overlooks the statement about the reckoning of faith as righteousness (Gen. 15:6). This shows he is not relying on the Pauline interpretation of Abraham's story, but is rather developing his thoughts independently of Paul. He is concerned with presenting a series of witnesses who have proven their faith in the history of God's people. The chain reaches from the beginning of creation to the members of the community who were perfected in suffering.

Faith shows its overcoming power by being persuaded of God's reality, which cannot be perceived by the senses. It is able to withstand the thought that there might be no God. It knows rather that God is a just judge and rewards each as he deserves (11:6). Thus it can stand up to the dangerous temptation brought on by the critical objections of atheism. The model of witnesses of faith guarantees that faith will also prove itself dependable in the future. Among them the figure of Abraham stands out. He was obedient to the call, left his home and went to a foreign land. But there, too, he remained a stranger, since he did not seek earthly security, but depended rather on the securely built city whose builder and maker is God (11:8-10). And when he was put to the most difficult test—having to offer up to God his only son—he did as he was commanded, since he was certain that God was able to raise men even from the dead (11:17-19). Thus he is an example and model of believers who perpetually are seeking the heavenly home (11:13-16). In Luther's lectures of 1517–18 on the Letter to the Hebrews, he said the following about this faith: "Precisely that is the glory of faith: Not to know where you are going, what you are doing, what you are suffering, to relinquish everything, feeling and understanding, being able and wanting—and to follow nothing but the voice of God, thus to let oneself be led and driven more than to drive oneself. And thus it is evident that Abraham gave us the highest model of a life according to the gospel with his obedient faith, since he left everything behind, followed only the Lord, preferred the word of God above all else, loved it above all else, was willingly a stranger and every hour subjected himself to dangers of life and death."[106]

The Letter to the Hebrews speaks of faith only in the sections that turn to the congregation with admonitions (3:7–4:13; 5:11–6:20; 10:19–13:17), not, however, in the doctrinal discussions that deal with the incomparable majesty of Christ. Thus it speaks about the steadfast power of the believers who never give in on the long sojourn of the people of God, but rather proceed undaunted toward the future peace promised by God (4:3). The letter recalls that through patient steadfastness faith becomes the heir of the Old Testament promises (6:11 ff), and it points to Abraham, who trusted in God's promise of blessing (6:13 ff). Faith perseveres in unbroken tenacity and relies in convinced certainty on the fact that God, who has given his promisory pronouncement, is true (10:22 ff).

Just as the apostle Paul, the author of the Letter to the Hebrews also speaks extensively about faith and emphasizes its incomparable importance. Its concept of faith, however, is not significantly different from the Pauline understanding. Whereas Paul designates faith as faith in Christ in the full sense, the Letter to the Hebrews describes faith as persevering loyalty to the object of hope. Since it is convinced of the reality of God's invisible world, it directs itself to the future goal. With this description of faith the Letter to the Hebrews draws from considerations it could have found in Jewish traditions. The Jewish philosopher Philo of Alexandria (see above p 105) attempted to understand faith as the turning to that which alone is truth and which stands above the world of creation.[107] "Whoever truly trusts in God (ie, believes God), that person has recognized that one cannot trust anything which is created and mortal. . . . But whoever succeeds in looking and stepping beyond all that is physical and nonphysical, and, with strong insight and unshakable trust, in finding his firm support alone in God, that person is in truth to be praised as happy and blessed."[108]

The Letter to the Hebrews presupposes these considerations as we find them presented in Philo, and from them develops its understanding of faith. To be sure, like the apostle Paul, the author emphasizes that faith does not stand at the end of a pious life as the highest virtue, but rather at the beginning of the Christian's life. Like Philo, however, the Letter to the Hebrews stresses that faith does not direct itself toward earthly events, but rather toward the future world. Jesus is placed before the community as the pioneer and perfecter of faith (12:2), thus showing the community the direction and goal of the path they are to embark upon and continually follow. If they will look to Christ, who has gone before them, and continue along the path he has prepared for then, then in the end the believers will receive the fullness of salvation as heirs of the promise.

V. The Johannine Writings: Faith and Knowledge

1. Belief in Jesus' Word

In the Fourth Gospel and the Johannine Letters, the latter of which were probably not composed by the evangelist, but came rather from his circle of pupils, only the verb "to believe" is used throughout the Greek text; the only exception is 1 John 5:4, where the noun "faith" is mentioned. The act of believing fills all areas of the life and action of the Christian as a powerful moving force. [109] At the end of his own book the evangelist says it was written "that you may believe that Jesus is the Christ, the Son of God, and that believing you may have life in his name" (20:31). And right at the beginning he emphasizes that John the Baptist was sent by God in order to witness to the light "that all might believe through him" (1:7). Jesus' effect is thus represented from the beginning to the end as a proclamation which calls one to faith. In this process the account of Jesus' words and acts is much more tightly combined into a unity with the confession of the Christian community than in the other Gospels. What Jesus says is nothing other than the proclamation of the crucified and risen Christ, and what he does is nothing other than the act of God, which acts through the Spirit. Thus the gospel is understood as a confessing testimony which would like to awaken faith, since it does not find its corresponding answer in an interested attentiveness, but rather only in faith. The ancient church gave the Fourth Evangelist—whose name has remained unknown—the designation "the theologian" and thus adequately emphasized that his work is carried by the reflecting power of faith. It is thought to develop the testimony of Christ as it discloses itself to the faith in Jesus' glory. Jesus' acts are signs in which his glory becomes manifest; and his words, which unambiguously clarify the meaning of his acts, show that salvation and deliverance are given in him alone.

In many passages the evangelist draws on the general language usage of early Christianity. Faith is related to Christ, the Son of God. It is thus either described with the short phrase "faith in Jesus" (3:16; 4:39; 8:45 ff; 12:44; 14:1; 17:20; and elsewhere) or with a "that" sentence in which the reference of faith is explained more clearly (6:69; 11:27, 42; 17:8; and elsewhere). The believers confess that the Father sent the Son into the world (5:24; 10:37 ff; 11:42; 17:8, 21; and elsewhere). When Jesus directs the question to his disciples concerning whether they, like the others who have turned away from him also want to go forth (6:67), Peter answers as spokesman for the circle of disciples, "Lord, to whom shall we go? You have the words of eternal life; and we have believed, and have come to know, that you are the Holy One of God" (6:68 ff). Overcome by Jesus' words, faith receives the certainty that Jesus is the one sent by God and as the Holy One, belongs wholly to God. He speaks the Father's word and does his work. Whoever trusts him believes in him and thus also in God. All who believe in Jesus' words understand that he is speaking as the Son of the Father, since—as the Johannine Christ says—"He who believes in me, believes not in me but in him who sent me" (12:44).

This faith must protest itself against falsification of its content and thus reject gnostic heresies. The First Letter of John disputes the view that Christ only seemingly became man, and in truth remained a heavenly spiritual being. Jesus' humanity is emphatically stressed because redemption depends on his suffering, dying, and resurrection. Those who deny

Jesus is the Christ are thus called liars (1 John 2:22). The Spirit of God, however, is recognized in the confession "that Jesus Christ has come in the flesh" (1 John 4:2; cf also 4:15; 5:1,5; 2 John 7). This faith possesses overcoming power that conquers the world's hostility and darkness and holds fast to the communion with God. In this way faith wins a part in the victory with which Christ overcame the world and becomes master over fear and dread (John 16:33).

In the Johannine writings the word faith can also be used without a more specific designation, though this does not result in a change in its meaning, because faith's christological reference is maintained unambiguously throughout. Thus it is said that many Samaritans believed in Jesus (4:39). A bit later, however, we read that the Samaritans say to Jesus: "It is no longer because of your words that we believe, for we have heard for ourselves, and we know that this is indeed the Savior of the world" (4:42). And at the end of the story that tells of the healing of the man born blind and of his encounter with Jesus, the author tells us further that the healed man recognized who Jesus was and spoke: "Lord, I believe" (9:38). That means, however: he has understood that Jesus is the Son of man whom God has sent into the world (9:35-37).

Faith arises from hearing Jesus' words (2:22; 4:39, 41 ff, 50; 5:24, 47; 8:31; 10:25; 12:36) and from seeing his deeds (2:11, 23; 5:36-38; 10:38; 14:11). Simple faith in miracles, however, aroused under the impression of extraordinary occurrences, is not real faith; it remains attached to superficial appearances and is dependent on the signs and miracles it has experienced (4:48; cf also 6:26, 36). That kind of faith can at best be considered incomplete and preliminary (1:50; 2:11, 23-25; 4:48; 7:31; 20:29). Only when faith, which grows from what is visible, directs itself to Jesus' word and trusts him, does it become changed into genuine faith (4:50, 53).[110] Jesus' signs are to be taken as signs pointing out that he is the bread of life (6:35, 48,

51), the light of the world (8:12), the resurrection and the life (11:25). Wherever these signs are understood, the decision of faith has been met (11:47 ff; 12:37). A faith that turns to Jesus no longer demands that he prove himself through signs in such a way that no doubt is raised concerning his claims; such faith rather directs itself to his pronouncement and puts all its trust in it. It understands that "blessed are those who have not seen and yet believe" (20:29).

All who hear Jesus' words are challenged to answer him. Each person carries the responsibility for his own answer, so that believing assent can be designated as obedience, negating rejection as disobedience (3:36). Yet no matter how clearly one is called to make the right decision, it is equally clear that faith can never be a work or act of merit for man. Every one who is of the truth can hear Jesus' voice (18:37). Only then, when the Father draws men to Jesus (6:44) and brings them to Jesus (10:29), do they come to have faith in him. That coming to Jesus and the Father's active drawing, however, are not connected in the sense that the one is complemented by the other so that both work together. God's drawing men to Jesus occurs in the answer of faith with which they take up Jesus' call and come to him. Faith thus understands that it is not thrown back on itself, but is rather grounded in God.

In the rejection Jesus experiences everywhere, one can recognize the judgment of divine hardness which results in men not being able to believe (12:37-40). All those who are of the world—that is, are determined by this world and who put their trust only in what is accessible—do not comprehend who Jesus is. Thus they miss life because they are caught in lies (8:44, 55) and because Jesus speaks nothing other than the truth (8:46) which he himself is (14:6). On the other hand, the miracle of faith occurs again and again, faith which accepts the invitation by the power of divine mercy: "While you have the light, believe in the light, that you may become sons of light" (12:36).

2. Remaining in Faith

Faith is not exhausted in the one-time answer given to Jesus' word, but rather determines the believer's entire life. Thus it is important that faith follow Jesus' words (8:51; 14:23; 15:20; 17:6), or—as one can also express it—that it remain in his word. In the Johannine words which speak about this constancy, Jesus' disciples are, as it were, shown the place where they are to stand and act from now on.[111] A person remaining in the word is told that he will know the truth (8:31 ff).

Knowing and believing are frequently mentioned together in the Fourth Gospel, and when this is done there is no distinction made between the object of knowledge and that of faith. Just as one believes that the Father has sent Jesus (11:42; 17:8, 21), so also does one know that the Father is the only true God and that he has sent Jesus (17:3). One comprehends in knowing (7:17) as well as in believing (16:27-30) that Jesus' teaching comes from the Father. If, on the one hand, truth is the object of knowledge (8:32), then, on the other hand, faith understands that Jesus is the truth (14:6). One believes he is the Christ (11:27; 20:31), but one also knows it: "We have believed, and have come to know, that you are the Holy One of God" (6:69). Both terms stand next to each other in this sentence. This connection might suggest that faith is the first answer given in the encounter with Jesus, and that knowledge refers to the progressive understanding of Jesus' mission. This assumption is controverted, however, by the fact that in other passages the terms are presented in reverse order; that is, the author first speaks about knowing, and only then about believing (16:30; 17:8). The sentence "We know and believe the love God has for us" (1 John 4:16) almost sounds like an echo of Peter's confession, except that it speaks first of knowing, then of believing. Thus faith cannot be designated as the beginning and knowledge as its continuation. Both terms rather belong together in a way such that all believing should become a knowing, and all knowing which begins with faith should remain in faith.[112]

There can never be a progression that leaves faith behind and is nothing more than pure knowing. Being a Christian always takes place in faith that remains in Jesus' word. To be sure, faith always seeks to comprehend in knowledge what it believes, and in reverse fashion there can be no true knowledge that is not simultaneously faith. Knowledge is thus a "structural moment of faith."[113] Faith gives an answer to Jesus' words and work, and at the same time inquires about its meaning and significance, which it comprehends in knowledge. Knowing does not, however, take place in the investigation of argumentative proofs, but rather in a reflective consideration of faith. Just as faith is directed to knowledge, so also does knowledge remain perpetually related to faith. If faith has understood that the divine word has become man, and if it recognizes God's glory in the humbled one (1:14), then it will also remain aware that it cannot have this word in any other way than in the words of the Christian proclamation.[114]

3. Faith and Eternal Life

Only when the divine glory fulfills everything will knowing be transfigured into a vision of the glory the Father has given the Son (17:24). Faith, however, has already recognized that Jesus possesses words of eternal life (6:68), indeed, that he himself is the resurrection and the life (11:25), the way, the truth, and the life (14:6). That eternal life of which the Fourth Gospel speaks does not begin only in some world beyond, but means rather the life that is bequeathed here and now to the believers. If in Pauline theology salvation is described as the righteousness faith receives from God's mercy, then in the

Johannine writings the corresponding idea is the life given to faith. Christ is the life which no death can kill. Thus Jesus' pronouncement holds true: "Truly, truly, I say to you, he who hears my word and believes him who sent me, has eternal life; he does not come into judgment, but has passed from death to life" (5:24). Death, judgment, and resurrection are not described as future events that will come to pass at the end of time; the entire change occurs wherever Jesus' words are accepted in faith.[115] Whoever sees the son and believes in him, has eternal life (6:40, 47).

According to the understanding of the Johannine Gospel, the eschatological crisis is already happening in the present. The Father did not send the Son in order to judge the world, but rather so that the world might be saved through him (3:17). If he is turned away, there remains darkness and death. On the other hand, wherever he is accepted one finds light and life. Within this context there thus occurs that final separation, which simultaneously occurs as judgment. "He who believes in the Son has eternal life; he who does not obey the Son shall not see life, but the wrath of God rests upon him" (3:36; cf also 3:18). The decision concerning eternal damnation or eternal life is not made at some future day of judgment, but right now. "He who rejects me and does not receive my sayings has a judge; the word that I have spoken will be his judge" (12:47 ff).[116]

That step from death to life, from darkness to light is already taken through the answer of faith, since Christ is the resurrection and the life. Whoever believes in him will live, even though he die. And every one who lives and believes in him will not die in all eternity (11:25). To be sure, even the believers must suffer physical death, but it has lost its power to separate them from God. Communion with Jesus cannot be destroyed by death, but rather gives to the believers life which is different from earthly existence in that it lasts forever. Thus faith is the victory which has overcome the world (1 John 5:4).

That eternal life received by faith is filled with love.[117]

Thus when the disciples remain associated with Jesus, this can also be characterized as remaining in his love (15:9 ff). Whoever believes in him stands in that love and is bound to the new commandment Jesus has given to those belonging to him to love one another (13:34; 15:12). Faith and love together can also be called the one commandment. "And this is his commandment, that we should believe in the name of his Son Jesus Christ and love one another, just as he has commanded us" (1 John 3:23). The love of the brothers to one another is grounded in the love Jesus sent to those belonging to him (15:11-17). Fulfilling this commandment is not difficult (1 John 5:3), since the power of love going out from Christ flows through the believers. It becomes visible in their love to one another that they have come out of death and into life (1 John 3:13). Just as unbelief is given over to death and darkness, so also does a person remain in death who withholds love from a brother and hates him (1 John 3:14). However, that faith which trusts in Jesus' words in full confidence shows its overcoming power in love. Thus one can recognize Jesus' disciples by the fact that there is love among them (13:35).

In the New Testament writings various images and concepts are used to describe the one faith that grows from the call of the gospel and recognizes the Christ of God in Jesus of Nazareth. Faith is clearly fixed by means of this determination of its content, and the various ways in which one speaks of it are thus related to a common point. Trust in God, confidence, constancy, and knowledge are given wherever faith trusts in Jesus' word, bases its hope in the crucified and risen Christ, and becomes active in love. It knows that it does not grow out from itself, but rather from the mercy of God which in Christ has turned itself to that faith. Thus it does not build upon its own power, but rather upon the deliverance Christ offers it. It knows itself to be addressed by Christ's message since through this word truth and life are offered. As Paul Tillich says, faith—as a profound involvement in that which concerns us unconditionally—is an act of the entire person and encompasses the whole man in every aspect. Faith is neither a procedure that takes place within a certain realm of the personality, nor is it an individual function within the totality of human existence. Rather, all human functions are united in the act of faith,[118] and all of life's realms are determined by the fact that the believer says, "I believe that Jesus Christ is my Lord."[119]

Martin Luther gives the following answer to the question "When do I then have faith?": "If I do not just believe that what God says is true, but rather put my trust in him, give myself to him and dare to act with him, and believe without any doubt that he will be with me and act just as one says. . . . Such a faith which takes that risk in God, just as it is said: be it in life or death, that faith alone makes a true Christian and attains from God everything it wants."[120] That reluctant apprehensiveness, however, which thinks this kind of faith is too sublime to comprehend and realize in one's own life, is given encouragement by Luther with the words reminding us that whoever puts his whole trust in Christ has full salvation. Nothing higher can happen to a person than that he has Christ and Christ has him. After all, "one person may understand Christ better than the other, as one who loves him more and believes in him more strongly, but he does *not* for that reason have more than the other. Christ is one Christ for all people, and he is the same in those things which belong to blessedness."[121]

Notes

1. Compare G. Ebeling, *Das Wesen des christlichen Glaubens* (Tübingen: ³1967), by the same author: "Was heisst Glauben?" in *Wort und Glaube*, III (Tübingen: 1975), pp 225-35; by the same author: *Was heisst: Ich glaube an Jesus Christus?* ibid, pp 270-308.

2. Compare Paul Tillich, *Wesen und Wandel des Glaubens* (Frankfurt: 1961), p 7; by the same author: *Gesammelte Werke*, VII (Stuttgart: 1970), pp 111 and 125; see also D. Lührmann, *Glaube im frühen Christentum* (Gütersloh: 1976), pp 9-16.

3. We will not offer an investigation or presentation of the Hebraic term here. On the one hand there are several excellent studies to which one can refer. On the other hand the term "to believe" extends in the Old Testament far beyond the use of any one specific term, and in any case is thoroughly discussed in only a few passages. In this context—and concerning faith in the Old Testament in general—cf G. von Rad, *Theol. d. Alten Testaments* (⁴1965), p 402 ff. Eng. tr. Old Testament Theology (Harper & Row, 1962). Among the terminological investigations we should particularly mention the following works: A. Weiser, *Theolog. Wörterbuch zum Neuen Testament*, VI (1959), pp 182-91; H. Wildberger, *Theol. Handwörterbuch z. Alten Testament*, I (1971), cols 187-93; H. Wildberger, "Glauben," Erwägungen zu *h'mjn*, FS Baumgartner (1967), pp 372–86 (bibliog.), R. Smend, *Zur Geschichte von h'mjn*, ibid. pp 284-90.

4. Concerning the differentiation of the various editorial strata in the Pentateuch (the first five books) cf the commentaries (see nn 6 and 7). One normally distinguishes three continuing, and to a large extent parallel, presentations which are the results of editorial work in the Pentateuch: The Yahwist (tenth Century), the Elohist (ninth or eighth Century)—both named after their respective characteristic employment of God's name—as well as the Priestly writing (probably sixth Century). The contents and dating of these sources have recently been more seriously discussed (even to the point of maintaining they are not connected presentations); cf especially H. H. Schmid, *Der sogenannte Jahwist* (1976); R. Rendtorff, "Das überlieferungsgeschichtliche Problem des Pentateueh," *BZAW* 147 (1977). Nonetheless, the traditional view of the Pentateuch problem appears to me to be the most persuasive hypothesis within the broader context, in spite of some limitations.

5. Compare O. H. Steck, "Gen. 12:1-3 und die Urgeschichte des Jahwisten," in *Probleme biblischer Theologie: Festschrift G. von Rad zum 70. Geburtstag* (München:1971), pp 525-54.

6. Concerning the relationship between primal history and patriarchal history, cf especially G. v. Rad, "Das erste Buch Mose," ATD 2/4 (⁹1972), pp 116 ff; 121 ff; H. W. Wolff, "Das Kerygma des Jahwisten, in Ges. Stud. z. AT, *ThB* 22 (1964), pp 345 ff, particularly 351 ff; O. H. Steck *op cit*.

7. Compare H. Gunkel, *Genesis* (HK) and G. v. Rad *op cit*.

8. With W. M. Clark, *VT* 21 (1971), pp 261-80 and C. Westermann, *Genesis BK I*, p 573.

9. Compare V. Maag, "Der Hirte Israels," *Schweizerische Theol. Umschau* (1958), pp 2-28; by the same author, "MALKUT JHWH," *SVT* VII (1960), pp 129-53.

10. There are, however, important arguments to the contrary; cf already P. Volz/W. Rudolph, "Der Elohist als Erzähler—ein Irrweg der Pentateuchkritik?" *BZAW* 63 (1933).

11. Compare O. Kaiser, *ZAW* 70 (1958), pp 107 ff.

12. It remains uncertain whether there was once the beginning of a narrative at this point—perhaps the beginning of the Elohist-source; in any case, the text would now have a different position and function.

13. Compare G. v. Rad, "Das erste Buch Mose," p 142.

14. The "statements of faith" in Pss. 27:13, 116:10 and 119:66, formulated in the first person singular, come closest to this; there the trust maintained even in need is emphasized (Pss. 27:116) or else confidence in Yahweh's (saving) commandments is expressed.

15. *Zwei Glaubensweisen* (1950).

16. *Op cit,* p 6.

17. *Ibid.*

18. M. Buber, *op cit,* pp 42 ff, must admittedly give a different interpretation. He writes: "It is now expected of Abraham that he 'trust God further' (this is to express the peculiar verb form)." Buber is here concerned about the "further," the continuation and continuity. But the translation is based on the firm conviction about the essence of Old Testament faith, and does not take the preceding text into consideration.

19. Concerning this: G. v. Rad, *Das Opfer des Abraham* (1971).

20. This same topic will be discussed in the section on the New Testament from a different perspective; thus one may cf pp 67 ff.

21. Concerning the specifics of differentiating between sources, see M. Noth, "Das zweite Buch Mose," *ATD* 5 (1959), pp 82 ff.

22. We do not, of course, know anything specific about the people's religious consciousness during the rescue; along with other historical models one could also imagine that Moses interpreted the deed for them as an act of Yahweh. That, however, changes nothing concerning the relationship between faith and miracle; it does not change the fact that faith can experience an historical event as a miracle. That is a question of the (precise) perception of the event, of apperception, and in that case it is insignificant in the final analysis whether such perception is simultaneous with the event. The important thing is that the perception be *true.*

23. According to H. Wildberger, *Theol. Handwörterb. zum Alten Testament,* I, col 193.

24. F. Nietzsche, *Also sprach Zarathustra,* Kröner Taschenausgabe (Stuttgart: 1964), p 98.

25. The question can remain open whether they once *were* of such use; they are not useless because they can be proven wrong, but because they do not correspond to the biblical understanding of God.

26. *Weimarer Ausgabe* 45, p 394.

27. An extensive collection of the various phrases can be found in H. Gunkel/J. Begrich, *Einleitung in die Psalmen* (1933, ³1975), pp 232 ff.

28. More specific material concerning this can be found in H.-J. Hermisson, "Sprache und Ritus im altisraelitischen Kult," *WMANT* 19 (1965), pp 113 ff.

29. J. W. Goethe, *Torquato Tasso* V, 5; in the form cited one finds it as the motto of the "Elegie," Artemisausgabe I, p 475.

30. Compare H. Vorländer, "Mein Gott. Die Vorstellungen vom persönlichen Gott im Alten Orient und im Alten Testament," *AOAT* 23 (1975).

31. Concerning this, see G. v. Rad, *Der Heilige Krieg im alten Israel* ([2]1952), pp 56 ff; *Theol. d. Alten Testaments*, II, pp 166-68. Concerning the translation and interpretation finally O. H. Steck, *EvTh* 33 (1973), pp 77-90. The translation of the saying is controversial, yet the question concerning the meaning of "faith" is hardly affected.

32. Compare O. H. Steck, *op cit.*

33. Concerning this compare also O. H. Steck, *ThZ* 29 (1973), pp 161-78.

34. Compare G. v. Rad, *Der Heilige Krieg im alten Israel* ([2]1952), pp 60 ff.

35. Concerning the exegesis cf *EvTh* 31 (1971), pp 672-74.

36. Concerning the delimitation of the pre-Pauline tradition cf the commentaries that deal with the passage, above all H. Conzelmann, *Der erste Brief an die Korinther* (Göttingen: 1969), and J. Jeremias, *Die Abendmahlsworte Jesu*, (Göttingen: [4]1967). pp 95-97; this also offers further secondary references.

37. Concerning the interpretation of the early Christian tradition against the background of its religious-historical presuppositions, cf E. Lohse, *Märtyrer und Gottesknecht* (Göttingen: [2]1963), pp 113-16.

38. Concerning the specifics and progression of the passion of Jesus cf E. Lohse, *Die Geschichte des Leidens und Sterbens Jesu Christi*, (Gütersloh: [2]1967).

39. Concerning the delimitation of the early Christian statement cf the commentaries that deal with the passage, above all E. Käsemann, *An die Römer*, (Tübingen: [3]1974), as well as P. Vielhauer, *Geschichte der urchristlichen Literatur* (Berlin: 1975), pp 29-32, and E. Lohse, *Entstehung des Neuen Testaments* (Stuttgart: [2]1975), p 21.

40. In theological language that means: The content of faith, which is characterized as *"fides quae creditur,"* and the execution of faith, which is called *"fides qua creditur,"* belong inseparably together. Compare R. Bultmann, *Theol. d. Neuen Testaments* (Tübingen: [6]1968), p 300; H. Conzelmann, *Grundriss der Theologie des Neuen Testaments* (München: [2]1968), Eng. tr. *Theology of the New Testament* [Scribners, 1970] pp 79 and 193.

41. Compare W. Kramer, *Christos Kyrios Gottessohn* (Zürich: 1963), pp 41-46.

42. Compare R. Bultmann, in *Theolog. Wörterbuch zum Neuen Testament*, VI, p 218.

43. Compare P. Tillich, *Systematische Theologie* III (Stuttgart: 1966), pp 155, 157. Eng. Tr. *Systematic Theology*, III (University of Chicago: 1976).

44. Compare A. Schlatter, *Der Glaube im Neuen Testament* (Stuttgart: [4]1927), pp 243 ff.

45. Compare D. Lührmann, "Pistis im Judentum," *Zeitschrift für die neutestamentliche Wissenschaft* 64 (1973), pp 19-38, as well as his book *Glaube im frühen Christentum* (Gütersloh: 1976), pp 31-45. Concerning this as well as what follows, see E. Lohse, "Emuna und Pistis—Jüdisches und urchristliches Verständnis des Glaubens," *Zeitschrift für die neutestamentliche Wissenschaft* 68 (1977), pp 147-63.

46. *Contra Apionem* II 169.

47. Compare the article by Lührmann (n 45) and H. Braun, *Wie man über Gottnicht denken soll, dargelegt an Gedankengängen Philos von Alexandria* (Tübingen: 1971), particularly pp 79-94.

48. *Leg. All.* II 89.

49. The so-called Hellenistic-Jewish missionary literature was in general primarily dedicated to this task. Compare P. Dalbert, *Die Theologie der hellenistisch-jüdischen Missionsliteratur* (Hamburg: 1954).

50. Compare Lührmann, *op cit*, p 34.

51. This is what one finds in the Midrash to the book of the prophet Habakkuk, 1 QpHab VIII, 1-3 and elsewhere.

52. Compare W. G. Kümmel, "Der Glaube im Neuen Testament," in *Heilsgeschehen und Geschichte*. Gesammelte Aufsätze 1933-1964 (Marburg: 1965), pp 67-80, particularly p 68.

53. Compare R. Bultmann, in *Theolog. Wörterbuch zum Neuen Testament* VI, pp 178 ff.

54. In older religious-historical scholarship the view was that the demand of faith was brought into the central position of the salvation message in the syncretistic religions of later antiquity (see R. Reitzenstein, *Die hellenistischen Mysterien-religionen* (Leipzig: ³1927), pp 234-36 Eng. tr. *Hellenistic Mystery-Religions* (Pittsburgh Theological Monograph: 1978). Nonetheless; this assumption does not hold true for the pre-Christian period, since there are no proof-texts as yet which can support the view (cf Lührmann, op cit, pp 21-24). One hears talk about the salvation power of faith in the Mystery religions of later antiquity only after the dispute with the Christian understanding of faith. We read, eg, in Celsus, who fought the Christians in the second century: "If you want to be saved, then believe" (Origenes, *Contra Celsum* VI, 11). And the Syrian writer Lucian, who also wrote in the second century and offers information about Christians as well as other religions, reports that at the beginning of the Mystery celebration one cried out: "If an atheist, Christian, or Epicurean has come to spy out this celebration, then he should flee! But those who believe in God should consecrate themselves with good fortune" (Lucian, *Alexander* 38; compare Vielhauer, *op cit*, p 38, n 71). In these phrases one unmistakably hears the echo of Christian terminology, which thus cannot be called a pre-Christian mode of expression.

55. Concerning the dispute that Jews and Christians had about the understanding of faith, compare M. Buber, "Zwei Glaubensweisen" (1950, in *Werke* I (München/Heidelberg: 1962), pp 651-782; and G. Ebeling, "Zwei Glaubensweisen?", in *Wort und Glaube* III (Tübingen: 1975), pp 236-45.

56. In this section only the First Three Gospels are discussed, which stand in a relationship of literary dependence and thus may be called synoptics. "Synopsis" means viewing together: if one orders the text of the First Three Gospels in columns next to each other, one sees that the Gospel of Mark is the oldest. The evangelists Matthew and Luke used it independently as a model. Beyond that they had one other source, which primarily contained words and sayings of Jesus—the so-called Sayings-source (Q = German *Quelle*, "source"). In a later section we will deal with the statements which the Gospel of John makes concerning faith. See below pp 109 ff.

57. Concerning the problem of how faith and history are related in the

Gospels. cf G. Bornkamm, *Jesus von Nazareth* (Stuttgart: ⁹1974), pp 11-23. Eng. tr. *Jesus of Nazareth* (Harper & Row, 1975).

58. Compare especially Luke 24:13-35 where it is shown how the risen Christ discloses the meaning of scripture; see E. Lohse, *Die Auferstehung Jesu Christi im Zeugnis des Lukasevangeliums* (Neukirchen: 1961).

59. Concerning this criterion, cf E. Lohse, *Grundriss der neutestamentlichen Theologie* (Stuttgart: 1974) pp 20-22; further secondary references are given there; concerning this entire group of problems see N. Perrin, *Was lehrte Jesus wirklich?* (Göttingen: 1972). Eng. tr. *Rediscovering the Preaching of Jesus* (Harper & Row, 1976).

60. Concerning this basic problem, cf E. Lohse, "Die Frage nach dem historischen Jesus in der gegenwärtigen neutestamentlichen Forschung" (1961), in *Die Einheit des Neuen Testaments* (Göttingen: 1973), pp 29-48.

61. This verse was later added to the parable of the two sons and is supposed to interpret this in the face of the differing behavior in reaction to the sermon of John the Baptist. Compare J. Jeremias, *Die Gleichnisse Jesu* (Göttingen: ⁸1978), p 78. Eng. tr. *The Parables of Jesus* (Scribner's, 1971).

62. Supporting texts can be found in P. Billerbeck, *Kommentar zum neuen Testament aus Talmud und Midrasch,* I (München: 1922), p 759.

63. Compare R. Bultmann, *Jesus* (Tübingen: ²1951), p 159; G. Bornkamm, *Jesus von Nazareth* (Stuttgart: ⁹1974), p 119; G. Ebeling, "Jesus und Glaube," in *Wort und Glaube,* I (Tübingen: ³1967), p 235.

64. Although nowhere in the New Testament surroundings is faith compared with the power which moves mountains, this graphic manner of speech surfaces twice later in the apocryphal Gospel of Thomas: "When you make the two one, you will become the sons of man, and when you say, 'Mountain, move away,' it will move away" (*Logion* 106); in the Nag Hammadi Library, ed. James M. Robinson (New York: 1977), p 129.

65. Supporting texts can be found in Billerbeck, *op. cit,* II (München: 1924), p 234.

66. In agreement with E. Schweizer, *Des Evangelium nach Matthäus* (Göttingen: 1973), p. 230 (Eng. tr. *The Good News According to Matthew* [John Knox, 1975]): Matt. 17:20 is allegedly the oldest form of the saying. Compare also G. Barth, "Glaube und Zweifel in den synoptischen Evangelien," *Zeitschrift für Theologie und Kirche* 72 (1975), pp 273 ff.

67. Within the context of the Gospel of Mark one might think here of the Mount of Olives.

68. Compare P. Fiebig, *Jüdische Wundergeschichten des neutestamentlichen Zeitalters* (Tübingen: 1911).

69. Compare R. Reitzenstein, *Hellenistische Wundererzählungen,* (Leipzig: 1906) (Darmstadt: ³1963); O. Weinreich, *Antike Wundertexte* (Berlin: 1960).

70. Compare R. Bultmann, *Die Geschichte der synoptischen Tradition* (Göttingen: ⁷1967), p 229. Eng. tr. *History of the Synoptic Tradition* (Harper & Row, 1963).

71. More recent compositions are found in the stories in Mark 10:46-52, par; Matt. 9:27-31, and Luke 17:11-19. In Mark 10:46 the name of the blind person is given; Matt. 9:27-31 can be recognized as a composition of the evangelist

Matthew; and Luke 17:11-19 is characteristically Lukan. Concerning the specifics cf Bultmann, *op cit*, pp 228 and 233.

72. Compare E. Käsemann, in *Die Religion in Geschichte und Gegenwart*, 3rd ed, II, col 995.

73. Compare H. J. Held, "Matthäus als Interpret der Wundergeschichten," in G. Bornkamm, G. Barth, H. J. Held, *Überlieferung und Auslegung im Matthäusevangelium* (Neukirchen: ⁶1970), pp 272-74.

74. This story does not constitute an historical account, but rather the Christian community's descriptive proclamation, which has Jesus encounter a Gentile; compare Bultmann, *op cit*, p 39.

75. Compare W. Schmithals, *Wunder und Glaube—eine Auslegung von Markus 4:35-6:6a* (Neukirchen: 1970), p 90.

76. As an introduction into Pauline theology see G. Bornkamm, *Paulus* (Stuttgart: ²1973). Eng. tr. *Paul* (Harper & Row, 1971).

77. In Gal. 1:23 Paul is alluding to a brief story which circulated among the Christians in Judea shortly after his conversion. "He who once persecuted us is now preaching the faith he once tried to destroy." Compare E. Bammel, Gal. 1:23, *Zeitschrift für die neutestamentlich Wissenschaft* 59 (1968), pp 108-12. The reference to faith here gives us the decisive differentiation from Judaism.

78. Concerning the significance of his conversion for Paul's theology, cf J. Jeremias, *Der Schlüssel zur Theologie des Apostels Paulus* (Stuttgart: 1971).

79. Concerning the prophetic understanding of the Pauline apostolic office, cf T. Holtz, "Zum Selbstverständnis des Apostels Paulus," *Theologische Literaturzeitung* 91 (1966), cols 321-330.

80. Compare E. Lohmeyer, "Probleme paulinischer Theologie I, Briefliche Grußüberschriften," *Zeitschrift für die neutestamentliche Wissenschaft* 26 (1927), pp 158-73, later in *Probleme paulinischer Theologie* (Darmstadt/Stuttgart: 1954), pp 9-29: Paul "is not the creator, but rather the continuation of an early Christian theology" (p 29).

81. Concerning the delimitation of the pre-Pauline piece, cf E. Käsemann, "Zum Verständnis von Röm 3:24-26 (1950/51)," in *Exegetische Versuche und Besinnungen* I, (Göttingen: ⁶1970), pp 96-100; E. Lohse, *Märtyrer und Gottesknecht* (Göttingen: ²1963), pp 149-54, by the same author, *Entstehung des Neuen Testaments* (Stuttgart: ²1975), pp 24 ff; Vielhauer, *op cit*, p 22; P. Stuhlmacher, "Zur neueren Exegese von Röm 3:24-26," in *Jesus und Paulus, Festschrift für W. G. Kümmel* (Göttingen: 1975), pp 315-33.

82. Compare H. W. Heidland, *Die Anrechnung des Glaubens zur Gerechtigkeit* (Stuttgart: 1936); by the same author, *Theolog. Wörterbuch zum Neuen Testament*, IV, pp 292-95.

83. *Virt.* 216; cf also *Op. Mund* 170-72; and see L. Goppelt, *Theologie des Neuen Testaments*, II (Göttingen: 1976), pp 454 ff.

84. *Virt.* 211-15.

85. Compare above pp 13 ff and E. Käsemann, "Der Glaube Abrahams in Röm 4" in *Paulinische Perspektiven*, (Tübingen: ²1972), pp 140-77. Eng. tr. *Perspectives on Paul* (Fortress, 1971).

86. Compare E. Lohse, "Die Gerechtigkeit Gottes in der paulinischen Theologie," in *Die Einheit des Neuen Testaments* (Göttingen: 1973), pp 209-27, particularly p 214.

87. Compare K. Kertelge, *Rechtfertigung bei Paulus* (Münster: 1967), p 193.

88. Thus reads the second benediction of *the Jewish Prayer of 18/18 Prayer:* "Blessed be the true Judge, who causes death and life."

89. "Erbauliche Auslegung des Alten Testaments," in *Mekh Ex 14:31* (40*b*). Compare Billerbeck, *op cit*, III (München: 1926), p 200.

90. Concerning the relationship between Israel and Christendom, cf above p 106.

91. According to the Jewish religious philosopher Philo of Alexandria, on the other hand, faith stands as the highest virtue at the end of the path to God. Concerning his understanding of faith, cf above p 105 and R. Bultmann, in *Theolog. Wörterbuch zum Neuen Testament*, VI, pp 202 ff, p 218.

92. Compare E. Lohse, "Taufe und Rechtfertigung bei Paulus" (1965) in *Die Einheit des Neuen Testaments* (Göttingen: 1973), pp 228-44, particularly pp 243 ff.

93. Compare Bultmann, *op cit*, p 219.

94. M. Luther, *Vorlesung über den Römerbrief 1515–16* I (Darmstadt: 1960), pp 308-11. Eng. tr. *Lectures on the Epistle to the Romans* (Concordia, 1972).

95. Thus H. Braun, in *Die Religion in Geschichte und Gegenwart*, 3rd ed. II, col 1595.

96. Compare N. A. Dahl, *Die Theologie des Neuen Testaments, Theologische Rundschau* 22 (1954), p 44.

97. Concerning the doctrinal understanding of faith in the church of the second and third generation, cf R. Bultmann, *Theologie des Neuen Testaments* (Tübingen: ⁶1968), pp 487-89, 531-34.

98. Concerning this problem, cf in addition to the commentaries, particularly H. Windisch, "Zur Christologie der Pastoralbriefe," *Zeitschrift für die neutestamentliche Wissenschaft* 34 (1935), pp 213-38.

99. Compare E. Lohse, "Glaube und Werke—Zur Theologie des Jakobusbriefes" (1957), in: *Die Einheit des Neuen Testaments* (Göttingen: 1973), pp 285-306.

100. Concerning allusions to the one God in exorcism, see above p 118.

101. Compare G. Eichholz, *Jakobus und Paulus* (München: 1953); by the same author: *Glaube und Werk bei Paulus und Jakobus* (München: 1961); U. Luck, "Weisheit und Leiden. Zur Theologie des Jakobusbriefes," *Theologische Literaturzeitung* 92 (1967), cols 253-58; by the same author, "Der Jakobusbrief und die Theologie des Paulus," *Theologie und Glaube* 61 (1971), pp 161-79; W. Schrage, "Der Jakobusbrief," in H. Balz/W. Schrage, *Die katholischen Briefe* (Göttingen: 1973), pp 33-36: *Glaube und Werk bei Paulus und Jakobus.*

102. "Vorrede auf die Episteln des Jakobus und Judas," in Luthers Septemberbibel von 1522.

103. Compare Schrage, *op cit*, pp 5 and 36.

104. *Weimarer Ausgabe* 40 I, p 447: "*Fide autem nobis iustificatis, egredimur in vitam activam.*"

105. Concerning this general context cf E. Gräßer, *Der Glaube im Hebräerbrief* (Marburg: 1965) as well as G. Bautzenberg, "Der Glaube im Herbräerbrief," *Biblische Zeitschrift* NF 17 (1973), pp 161-77.

106. M. Luther, Vorlesung über den Hebräerbrief 1517/18, deutsche Übersetzung von E. Vogelsang (Berlin/Leipzig: 1930), p 173.

107. Compare D. Lührmann, "Pistis im Judentum," *Zeitschrift für die*

neutestamentliche Wissenschaft 64 (1973), pp 19-38, particularly p 29, and above p 104.

108. Philo, *Quis rerum divinarum heres sit* 93 ff. Compare A. Strobel, *Der Brief an die Hebräer* (Göttingen: 1975), p 210.

109. Concerning the term faith and its understanding in the Johannine writings, cf R. Bultmann, in *Theolog. Wörterbuch zum Neuen Testament* VI, pp 224-30; by the same author, *Theologie des Neuen Testaments* (Tübingen: ⁶1968), pp 422-45; H. Braun, in *Die Religion in Geschichte und Gegenwart*, 3rd ed, II, cols 1596 ff; R. Schnackenburg, *Das Johannesevangelium* I (Freiburg: ³1972), pp 508-24: *Das joh. Glauben;* S. Schulz, *Das Evangelium nach Johannes* (Göttingen: 1972), pp 197-200: *Wort und Glaube;* Lührmann, *op cit* (n 2), pp 60-69.

110. Compare E. Schweizer, "Die Heilung des Königlichen": Joh 4:46-54 (1951) in *Neotestamentica* (Zürich: 1963), pp 407-15.

111. Compare J. Heise, Bleiben. *Menein in den Johanneischen Schriften* (Tübingen: 1967), particularly p 174.

112. Compare R. Bultmann, in *Theolog. Wörterbuch zum Neuen Testament* VI, p 229.

113. Compare Bultmann, *ibid* and *Theol. d. Neuen Testaments*, p 426.

114. Compare E. Käsemann, *Jesu letzter Wille nach Johannes 17* (Tübingen: 1966, ³1971), pp 90 ff.

115. Concerning the eschatology of the Fourth Gospel, cf R. Bultmann, "Die Eschatologie des Johannes-Evangeliums," in *Glauben und Verstehen*, I (Tübingen: ²1954), pp 134-52: L. van Hartingsveld, *Die Eschatologie des Johannesevangeliums* (Assen: 1962); J. Blank, *Krisis, Untersuchungen zur johanneischen Christologie und Eschatologie* (Freiburg: 1964); P. Ricca, *Die Eschatologie des Vierten Evangeliums* (Zürich: 1966); there one will find further secondary references.

116. The reference "on the last day" should be considered a later addition by means of which the eschatology of the Fourth Gospel was to be accomodated to the contemporary ecclesiastical expectation of the end-time.

117. Concerning the concept of love in Johannine theology, cf finally M. Lattke, *Einheit im Wort: Die spezifische Bedeutung von "agape", "agapan" und "filein" im Johannes-Evangelium* (München: 1975).

118. Compare P. Tillich, *Wesen und Wandel des Glaubens* (Berlin: 1961), p 12.

119. Compare Martin Luther's explanation in the smaller catechism.

120. *Weimarer Ausgabe* VII, p 215.

121. *Weimarer Ausgabe* X, 1, 2, p 82.